Merlin Awakes

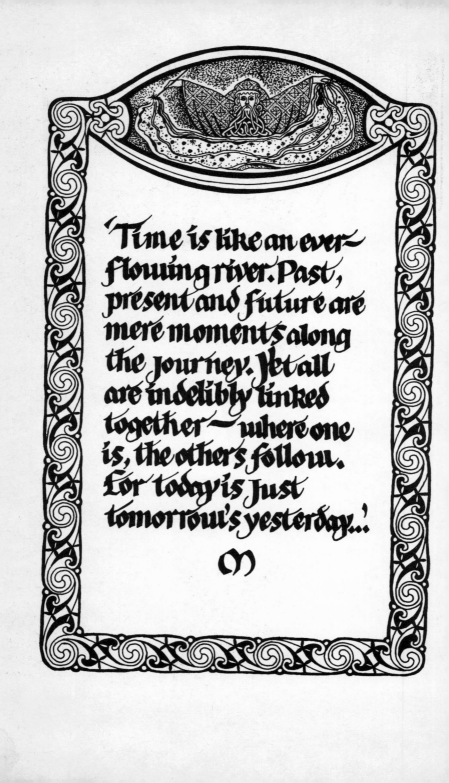

'Time is like an ever-flowing river. Past, present and future are mere moments along the journey. Yet all are indelibly linked together — where one is, the others follow. For today is just tomorrow's yesterday...'

M

Merlin
Awakes

Revelations and Truths for A New Age

PETER QUILLER

Illustrated by Courtney Davis

Firebird Books

First published in the United Kingdom in 1990 by
Firebird Books Ltd
P.O. Box 327, Poole, Dorset BH15·2RG

Distributed in the United States by
Sterling Publishing Co, Inc.
387 Park Avenue South, New York, N.Y. 10016-8810

Distributed in Australia by
Capricorn Link (Australia) Pty Ltd.
P.O. Box 665, Lane Cove, NSW 2066

British Library Cataloguing in Publication Data
Quiller, Peter, 1944–
    Merlin awakes.
    1. Self – discovery
    I. Title
    158.1

ISBN 1 85314 148 8 (hardback)
        1 85314 149 6 (paperback)

Designed by Kathryn S.A. Booth
Typeset by Inforum Typesetting, Portsmouth
Printed and bound in Great Britain by Biddles of Guildford

Contents

Acknowledgements

I would like to thank the following friends for their invaluable support in the compilation of this manuscript: Roy Davis; Debbie Rice; Toni Abdey; Michael Mann; Linda Coyle; Robert Chalcroft; Michael Stone; Christine Haesler; Shaun Thorpe; Terry Utting; Nicholas Ayres; and many other good friends and correspondents.

I should particularly like to thank Courtney Davis for his outstanding artwork.

I must thank Michael Joseph for all his encouragement, editorial services and constructive assistance in the compilation of the manuscript.

To my dear wife I must offer a very special vote of thanks for her love and patience, and for preparing me for my quest. I must thank her also for accompanying me on as much of it as time and circumstances allowed.

Finally, I must offer my thanks to the four Guardians – the King; the Mystic; the Holy Lady and the Magician. In particular I must thank 'Merlin', for without *him* none of this would have happened!

PETER QUILLER

Introduction

For many months the question plagued me: 'How should I begin this book?' I realised if I made a slapdash attempt to explain the many beautiful things that had happened to me, then the hard-nosed among you would sneer, cynically, and dismiss me as a 'head-case'!

I did not want to give that impression. Nevertheless, I was aware that I had to make the reader conscious of how difficult it was for me to share the personal revelations and transcendent experiences that are contained in this book. They are both delicate and vulnerable, particularly in the public forum. The reader should understand that I do not offer them up lightly or easily.

It is with great caution, therefore, that I begin by stating that this book is about – truth.

One may then ask what truth? I would answer: Great Truth.

For me, it was a revelation to discover that one finds such truth only through mystical experience. There is no easier way to it; in fact there *is* no other way to it! Ironically, once discovered, one cannot contain this Truth, or own it, for it slips away from the grasp should one attempt to capture it or cling on to it. One simply has to acknowledge its existence. Once accomplished, the long-term effects of such an acceptance can be awesome and magical.

It was through such magic that is contained in the Arthurian Romances that I began my search. They contain a 'doorway' through which one can pass towards a greater personal understanding. There are many doors and many pathways, and this book is about my search and what happened to me along the Way.

'Now I a fourfold vision see,
And a fourfold vision is given to
me;
'Tis fourfold in my supreme delight
And threefold in soft Beulah's night
And twofold always. May God us
keep
from single vision and Newton's
sleep...'

William Blake

Merlin Awakes

Prior to the early 1970s, I had no interest whatsoever in the Arthurian romances. If I had given them any attention at all, I would have considered they had no bearing on the present day. How wrong I was. Certain events that happened to me during the latter half of the seventies changed my thinking dramatically.

It all began early in 1975. I awoke on a mid-March night, within days of the Spring equinox, at three o' clock in the morning – which, by coincidence, was my birth-time. The bed seemed to be swinging from side to side; my head was spinning; it felt as if only the weight of the bedclothes was preventing me from floating up to the ceiling!

No, I had not been drinking! I could hardly believe my eyes. There, in the centre of the bedroom, floated a wide band of purple 'light energy' reaching from floor to ceiling. Within this subtle purple force shone a myriad gold and silver pinpoints of light that swirled about like constellations in miniature. I gaped at this vision in amazement whilst it lit up the bedroom. Growing rather alarmed, I felt obliged to challenge it in some way:

"Who the hell are you?"

"WHAT IS IN A NAME?" A deep booming voice echoed in my ears in answer to my question.

"That's all very well," I retorted, rather lamely, "but who are you and what are you doing in my bedroom?"

"If you *must* have a name, call me – 'Merlin'."

I was speechless. The enormity of the situation began to dawn on me and I gawked in astonishment at the brilliant vision. I was fascinated to notice how the dancing constellation lights seemed to pulse in rhythm with the voice as 'it' spoke. I estimated that the purple column must be at least eight feet across, as the wide window at the eastern end of the room was completely obscured by it. Top and bottom seemed to disappear into the floor and ceiling, so it must have been at least eight feet in height too. The edges of the energy field were indeterminate for the purple seemed to fade into the walls rather than produce a sharply defined line. It felt 'enormous'. It was as if the energy was squeezing a fraction of itself into the room. The purple was brightest in the middle of the column, where the constellations were most densely packed together and in constant motion. I pinched myself very hard, more than once, to see if I was dreaming.

After allowing me time for reflection the voice spoke again:

"You have nothing to fear from me," it said. "We are old

friends. We have worked together many times. Now you will begin to remember me . . . "

There was a brilliant flash from the energy column, followed by a short, blinding pain in my head. Then, a wonderful feeling of peace pervaded my whole being; I luxuriated in it. Strangely, I did begin to sense a feeling of familiarity as the voice of 'Merlin' continued:

"You may call upon me at any time, although I may not always be able to respond directly like this; make good use of the times we *do* have together . . . "

I managed to mumble a hasty "thank you" which was greeted by rich resonant laughter that slowly faded away in a procession of echoes.

"You have much to learn," said Merlin. "Remember, you will always be able to recognise my presence through the physical sensations you are experiencing at this moment. In future they will not be as intense, but you will know when I am around. We have much to discuss. Not all will believe you when you report our conversations; some may not trust the source. No matter, you will not fail . . . "

There were further rich cadences of laughter and then the energy started to fade. I fell back to sleep after a few minutes, totally dumbfounded by the whole experience, and yet curiously at ease with the concept of meeting *him* again.

It took me quite a while to come to terms with this new energy in my life! Rationally, I first thought it had all been a dream. However, things began to happen which seemed to confirm the reality of the incident. Books and audio tapes arrived that I had not ordered but which had a definite connection with the Arthurian romances. For example, the first of Mary Stewart's trilogy of books about Merlin, plus Rick Wakeman's recording *King Arthur and the Knights of the Round Table* came to the door within hours of the first energy manifestation.

From the beginning, Merlin appeared as an energy rather

than as a solid, identifiable individual. I soon found an excellent place where I could call on him – the enormous oak tree at the edge of our garden. At certain times, the oak seemed to act as a channel for communication. In our dialogues Merlin suggested we use a code system as a means of identification between us. If other people came to see me and quoted one of these codewords, or 'call-signs', in the course of casual conversation, I would realise that it was no accident their being there. From that mid-March night onward my life changed *absolutely*. It was as if the previous 'me' ceased to exist.

I had been a film cameraman for some years. Gradually, I began to lose interest in my occupation and started looking for something else from life. You might think me irresponsible, but I sincerely believed that my life had to change in some way. I wrote poetry for the first time and thoroughly enjoyed it; I started to read the classics again and found a new dimension in them; I began to walk everywhere and the pace of my life altered. At last I had some time to stand and stare! I went on long cross-country hikes; I developed an interest in old buildings, churches and the ancient landscape. I felt I was beginning to touch history in a way I had never done before. This involvement with everything around me was like waking from a dream and seeing clearly for the first time. I had been blind for years!

I found it easy to accept the concept of ley-lines, for there did appear to be subtle energies present in some locations that were absent from others. Indeed, I found there were discernible flows in the energies, for they seemed to wax and wane with the seasons, the moon, and even the people who sometimes accompanied me on my hikes! There are people, I have discovered, who can dramatically affect spiritual energy one way or another.

Merlin warned me about all kinds of strange characteristics and behavioural patterns that we humans possess and the defences we create around ourselves. Thus, in a sense, I was prepared for some of the peculiar reactions that I experienced later. He became a great teacher. We established a routine of master/pupil very early on in our dialogues; these conversations covered the widest and sometimes the most unexpected range of subjects. He even suggested which books I should read, often marching me up to them in bookshops and giving me a prod! Under his guidance, I became aware of the resurgence of interest in ancient sites and alignments that took place at the beginning of the twentieth century, and that the re-emergence of Merlin could be connected with this. I also discovered that the writings of John Cowper Powys, C.S. Lewis and J.R.R. Tolkien seem to reflect this reawakening of long-dormant energies.

Prompted by Merlin, I became acquainted with the work of such authors as Alfred Watkins, Guy Underwood, John Michell and T.C. Lethbridge, all of whom seemed to be convinced that something from the past was beginning to re-materialise; something that would reveal just how much more sensitive our so-called 'primitive' ancestors really were and how much more 'aware' they had been of subtle energies.

Merlin guided me to many ancient sites where I found there were subtle energies present – in some cases still active and in others dormant. These expeditions aroused my interest in the techniques of dowsing and healing and I soon learned that certain standing stones and crystals enhance this work.

Throughout our association, the Mage has continued to

explain many of the functions of awakening energies, often advising caution or attention to specific details. This led my wife to speculate that Merlin must have access to information far beyond the boundaries of the Earth. It has become clear to my wife and myself that 'Merlin' is merely one facet of a much greater whole. He has introduced us to other dimensions where we were able, briefly, to enter worlds that appear to co-exist with our own, beyond our familiar framework of space and time.

During his conversations, he revealed many of the ideas and comments that appear elsewhere in this book. He has helped me towards a much greater awareness; he has allowed me to feel that I could be of some use in the overall scheme of things. My first task was to begin working on myself. This has continued unchecked ever since, and I do not suppose it will ever be finished, though I have tried my best on rather intractable material!

Merlin has often stressed the importance of inner balance before one can attempt to assist in the distribution of higher energies on to the physical plane. He insists that we *are* on the threshold of a new beginning, but that each of us must put his own house in order before undertaking any Quest.

I find it hard to express just how much Merlin's guidance and friendship have meant to me for over fifteen years. His presence draws near, then recedes, in a cyclic fashion; but his advice is always available, should I need to call upon it, in this collection of his comments. He has inspired me with his words and his mere presence into realms of speculation far-removed from anything mundane. He has given me a glimpse of cosmic consciousness that boggles the imagination. His wisdom has fed the deeper recesses of my mind and made it come alive with vibrant new life. I think he is a representative of cosmic magic that has a universal appeal. His first visit was the beginning of a veritable symphony of energy that led me and my family to beautiful places in the

British Isles, where we met some amazing people. Merlin opened up the secret places of my heart and let in the light; in fact he almost broke my heart with the intensity of the various experiences he put in my way. I had some hard lessons.

Yet the beginning was mild when I look back to the garden and the oak tree and consider how far I have come since then.

'Our words are merely a means
to an end;
accept or reject them as you
will.
They come through a physical
channel and are, therefore,
subject to discolouration.
Visions cannot easily be
transferred to the page;
entire concepts may be taken
in at a glance, yet words are
needed to describe them —
and words are both limited
and limiting in their present
form.'

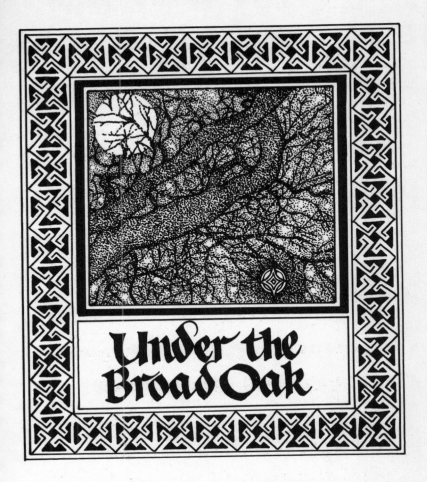

Under the Broad Oak

I have already hinted at how Merlin affected my reading. In fact, within hours of the first visit, Tolkien's *The Hobbit* and the *Lord of the Rings* began falling out of the bookcase until I finally relented and started to read them. The books proved to contain a wonderland of imagery that stirred vague memories within me, almost as if I had personal knowledge of the world Tolkien described. Looking back, I believe that what I was beginning to respond to was a deeper thread of meaning which is also contained in many other great works of fiction, art and music. Nevertheless, it took me a long time to begin to comprehend the sheer enormity of it. Clearly, the rôle of Merlin in all this was far more than that of an historical figure who had come, merely, to remind me of a 'golden era' of the past.

The discovery of the focal point under the oak tree was the start of this deeper voyage of understanding. What led me to it was the glimpsing of a child-like figure flitting around the end of our chicken-house. We had been experiencing a bit of trouble with youngsters stealing our eggs, so I was anxious to trap the villains in the act. I sped up the garden in hot pursuit, rounded the end of the hen-house to find – no-one! As there was nowhere for anyone to go from this position, without my having seen them, I was nonplussed. Then I became aware of a tinkling kind of laughter near our oak tree and turned around in time to see a slight, green-clad figure with a red hat disappear *into* the tree!

Logic told me I must be dreaming, but I went along with the vision and walked over to the tree. Within a few feet of it I started to experience the dizzy sensation that I recalled so well. I realised that I had been 'led' to the spot, presumably by one of the elf-like figures I had been reading about in the *Lord of the Rings*. I reasoned that this image must have been pulled out of my subconscious as it was something in which I was deeply immersed at the time. It served its purpose well. I recognised the connection between elves and trees that is an essential part of Lothlorien, a place of peace and mystical beauty. I was, therefore, susceptible enough to sense that such a spot had been created beneath our oak tree and this had to be the place where I could best communicate with my new-found friend.

In a matter of moments that deep, resonant voice echoed in my ears:

"Welcome, welcome, thrice welcome . . . "

This time there was no brilliant visual display. It was hardly necessary as the energy around the tree was so intense that I could touch it! I sat down among the tree roots and we began the first of many discussions that were to take place there over a period of years. Fortunately, at my wife's insistence, I was carrying with me a pad and pencil and I was able to record everything that was said as the first teaching session began.

Had anyone told me, a month or two previously, that one day soon I would be sitting beneath the oak tree in my garden, chatting with the wizard Merlin, I would have said that they were seriously disturbed! Yet here is the transcript of this first interchange where 'Q' indicates myself and 'M' is the Mage:

Q: "Why have you chosen *me* to talk to?"

M: "Why not?"

This set me back on my heels for a moment.

Q: "What do you want with me?"

M: "How many times do you have to be told? I have come to you for a purpose, to teach you and guide you. You have many tasks to accomplish in the future and you have completely disregarded all the other messengers we have sent!"

I sat silent, totally nonplussed by this remark, while that infectious laughter rolled around me like an enveloping blanket.

M: "I will lead you to certain books that I want you to read, as and when necessary. You have already seen an indication of my influence in this direction, have you not? (He chuckled again.) Do not clutter your mind with useless luggage! Learn to be far more discerning in what you read. I will teach you, but first I must ask one thing of you. Never use my name in full unless it is absolutely essential."

Q: "Why is that?"

M: "Certain spoken words contain an inherent power or energy that diminishes when they are bandied about thoughtlessly. By using the initial 'M' you will learn to appreciate the use of the full name far more. It will take on a deeper meaning for you in consequence. You will find that you can awaken trees with it and dormant energies too. But all that will come later. First we have much to discuss. Ask me the burning question that troubles you . . . "

I was astounded by this remark for I had wanted to ask a most important question that related to my childhood ambition to become a priest. Yet, I had been avoiding it for some reason.

I almost winced inwardly as I asked: "About Jesus?"

There was a momentary pause: "Jesus who?"

I felt strangely offended by this reply as I had expected a reprimand for my recent agnosticism, or at least a sermon extolling the virtues of Jesus. His reply, at first, seemed ridiculous.

I was making to get up and go back to the house when the Mage continued: "Consider this. What if Jesus had been a 'tempter' who succeeded? Try and come to terms with that!"

Q: "What do you mean? I am incredibly stupid, you must make things clear!"

M: "If Jesus had not existed, he would have been invented. Think on this well and we will talk some more very soon . . . "

I sat quietly while the energy around me swiftly dissolved. I was still sitting under the tree half-an-hour later when my wife called me in for lunch. Can you begin to imagine how I felt? In a few short sentences the Mage had shattered several major personal preconceptions. I understand how difficult it must be for anyone else to appreciate just how much the energy's presence affected me; but it was so powerful and loving that I implicitly trusted it. I was obliged, eventually, to alter my whole way of looking at the world and our conception of history as a result of these remarks. I had imagined that Merlin would go on at great length about Jesus and the tremendous impact of Christianity. Curiously, he had merely implied that all was not what it would seem to be. I could hardly wait for our next session. Sure enough, the energy was under the tree the following morning. We continued where we had left off:

Q: "May we talk some more about Jesus?"

M: "Of course . . . "

Q: "Remember what you said about Jesus? It has been driving me crazy! Can you *please* enlarge on that for me?"

There was a warmth exuded by the energy that is difficult to impart other than to describe it as an invisible 'smile'.

M: "It was the elevation of the Jesus figure to divine status that caused many problems. It is highly dangerous to deify any man, for God is *not* man. The conceit of certain members of the human race is beyond belief at times! 'Saint' Paul was a known misogynist, for example, and where do women figure in the legends of Jesus? In a subservient rôle of course! There have been many women 'messengers' in the past but all memory of them has been obliterated by priestly purges."

"There have been countless Christ-like figures in world history, both men and women. Each race or culture has its own Messengers of Truth and it is a measure of their success, or failure, how that message is received. 'Krishna', for example, is another word for Christ. Many religious leaders or teachers have been labelled thus; but remember it is only a label! Messengers are often sent to races who are lost, or advancing too quickly. They convey aspects of the Divine Truth, sometimes as a test."

"Consider why a message, ostensibly of peace, should suddenly become a message of force? There lies the distortion. GOD IS LOVE. Anything stemming from the higher planes of existence is infused with this energy, but the human receiver on the physical plane leaves much to be desired! As individuals you are isolated and many distortions of the loving energy have occurred, for no two people think exactly alike. A lot depends upon interpretation. People have preconceived ideas or forms that they slip around many of the 'visions' they receive. It is exactly the same with public heroes and heroines."

"Consider how much time had elapsed before the story of Jesus began to emerge. What folk call 'Christianity' today bears no relation to anything that took place two thousand years ago. The problems started with the person you choose to call 'Saint' Paul. He was employed to undermine and corrupt the new faith, and he did just that! *He* it was who first deified Jesus."

"Consider this: those who come to the physical plane with a specific spiritual purpose do not usually seek the centre of public gaze. Those whose work is of the highest order are rarely, if ever, noticed by the majority until their work is accomplished. Subsequently, their actions are often misinterpreted or worse, misrepresented. Generally, this will happen a long time after the actual events have taken place. Distortion often occurs when unscrupulous persons decide to utilise these figures for their own selfish purposes. Then what happens? Another 'idol' is created and added to the long list that mankind has adored throughout the ages! Ask yourself why it is that man needs the cult of the 'hero'? It is a strange flaw in your make-up and it is not an easy question to answer, given your present condition! Try and examine this idiosyncrasy from every angle; you will begin to see just what you are up against . . . "

My response to this was a long time coming: "You mean to say that I have to find the reason why the human race is so hero-fixated? Gosh! You don't expect much do you?"

M: "You must come to terms with this element of your-self. Examine it and find out why it exists. Why super-heroes? Why are they usually male? Remember, this is but one facet of a complex enigma! You will see just how com-plex as our association progresses. At this moment, I have become *your* super-hero. Think deeply on this . . . "

After this interchange my brain felt near to bursting with all the startling revelations. New concepts were swarming around in there like bees! I began to realise that I had led a totally blind existence until that moment. The Mage had begun to encourage me to start thinking responsibly for the first time in my life.

My young son approached us towards the end of this dialogue and I watched in amazement as his little face lit up on perceiving the energy all around me. He grinned hugely and waved up at someone or something I could not see.

"Stars!" he yelled, "Zoom! Zoom!"

He continued chuckling and gurgling as I held him close on my lap. I marvelled that he was so at home with the energy, and then I remembered how susceptible most children are to gentle, loving vibrations. What further proof did I need?

The energy dispersed slowly this time, leaving the pair of us gurgling happily together.

Since then I have received many confirmations from all kinds of sources reinforcing what the Mage explained about Jesus. The best-selling book *The Holy Blood and the Holy Grail* suggests a Jesus very different from the figure in the Bible. Donovan Joyce in *The Jesus Scroll* raises questions about the deification and resurrection of Jesus. There is even a current speculation that Jesus could have been black; and why not?

'For long ages we have been working towards a period when our powers will be taxed to the utmost'. It should come as no suprise, therefore, to learn that this period is now upon us...'

ℳ

24

Picking Up Good Vibrations

This seems to be the logical place in my narrative to pause for a moment and introduce the reader directly to the Magician's words without my presence intruding. In this way, I can let him speak directly to you. Arguably, the most important subject to emerge from our discussions has been that of the natural energy spectrum, and our abuse of it. Here, the Mage begins to enumerate our infamies and to indicate how best we can begin to readjust, collectively and individually. Try to imagine a very deep, resonant voice, full of rich cadences, that freely gives vent to emotion, and you will catch just an 'essence' of the original.

"There are many cycles of time emanating from the 'Great Year', or the Precession of the Equinoxes; these are sub-divided into ages, eons, millenia, etc. Every age contains an energy of its own that affects all those whose lifespans coincide with it. You are living in a time of great change and transformation."

"Many drastic changes have taken place in your world over the last one hundred and fifty years, but not all of them have been good ones. As Man's material conditions have improved, his spiritual aspirations have faltered and he has progressively lost sight of the debt he owes to the lovely planet that sustains him. No longer do the majority of you care and share – you selfishly grab and hoard with little thought for others, or for your future."

"Spaceship Earth has been pilotless for far too long. Indeed, some of your fellow crew members have forgotten so much about the direction and ultimate purpose of your flight that they are plundering the spaceship's stores in an orgy of self-indulgence. It is your individual duty to re-tune to the craft that is carrying you; to restore the sight of your fellows if you can. The Earth will soon pass on to your children; teach them to cherish and get to know their mother-ship."

"Become aware of the subtle energies flowing within, through and around you. Tune in to the energies that permeate the planet herself. Rediscover the ancient wisdom that your distant ancestors once acquired; blend with it the

26

highest achievements of today. This alchemy alone will put your spacecraft back on course, when once again it can resume its proper journey."

"Re-attune yourselves to the pulse of the Universe. It beats within all vibrations; everything is pervaded by it – even yourselves. You have simply ceased to hear it, to feel it within and around you. This heart-beat of the Universe pulses through all worlds seen and unseen. All living creatures gladly respond to it – except Man. Why are you so afraid? What have you got to lose?"

"Very soon information relating to energy sources at Earth nodal points will be released into the public consciousness. It will be the task of those of you who are attuned to such energies to spread the message of Light, Love and Peace throughout the darkness."

"It is vital that you rediscover the energies that your ancestors harnessed. In order for you to achieve this, you have to attain a harmony with the planet and with yourselves. Long periods of selective dieting, meditation and exercise will be necessary to reach a perfect balance within. You are not asked to aim for total perfection before embarking upon this work, but a right-minded attitude is essential."

"A positive frame of mind will be indispensable if you are to succeed. Be aware of your environment above all else, for it is this which sustains all living things and provides your every requirement for a healthy and balanced life. Abuse it at your peril!"

"The powers locked in the Earth are boundless. Even fossil fuels will become entirely unnecessary if you can harness these energies. Nuclear energy with active waste is not a safe way for the future. Fossil fuels are far safer at this time, until the 'new' energies are discovered."

"The atom has yet to reveal its creative aspects. Perhaps the unveiling of these powers will have to wait upon your greater maturity and discretion. Light, too, contains an energy you have yet to decipher."

"You are close to discovering techniques using sound in a variety of different disciplines but this will only begin to bear fruit when the crass exploitation of sound for military purposes ceases. Only then can the gentle, loving use of sound develop its full potential. Music can indeed be the 'food of love', for it paints pictures in the mind and can induce empathic vibrations with the higher worlds. Music should be used for the purposes of healing for it is a wonderful soporific, relaxing and soothing. Conversely, it can stimulate and exite emotions too."

"It is not always advisable to indulge in an *excess* of overloud music, no matter of what kind. This type of vibration serves to deaden the nerves and can destroy the perceptions completely in extreme cases, when taken to excessive levels. You can never hope to 'attune' yourself, or become aware of new vibrations, if your central nervous system is damaged or switched off! Uncontrolled sonics can be very dangerous."

"Positive efforts should be made in future to limit the use of sound for harmonious purposes only. You little realise the damage you wreak upon levels beyond your own, through the accidental creation of sonic imbalances."

"Prayer is a positive energy. Prayers for good and loving thoughts for the future should be at the forefront of your mind at all times. In the years ahead, caring vibrations of any kind will become increasingly important, and prayer is a powerful vibration. Try and become aware of the different types of energy that you emanate, create or share with those around you."

"The Earth is a living organism. Once you have grasped this fact you will begin to realise just how dependent upon her you really are, and how important it is for you to be in harmony with your Mother."

"Learn to draw energy from the awakening power centres, particularly for educative and healing purposes. Channel this energy to those who urgently need it."

"The power centres of the Earth work on higher vibrations. They serve to draw the light energy down into the physical plane, where it is most needed. Right-minded groups can help to spread these energies to where they can do the most good. However, the intentions of each individual undertaking such work will have to be totally unselfish, otherwise the energy will be wasted."

"The inner planes utilise these energies continuously. It is now incumbent upon you to bring them into play in the physical world if you are ever to avert the suicidal course of some of your fellows. The dangers in misusing the planet cannot be overstressed. She is your collective responsibility and must be respected. From now on, the Earth herself should be properly represented in your council chambers, if increasing confusion, hardship and peril are to be avoided."

"When we release new energies in to your world, extremes of all kinds occur; subtle emanations heighten all manner of emotions and pressures on the physical plane. Violence, often no more than a manifestation of Man's frustration, is one of the sadder, more negative aspects – as humankind strives to rediscover its true identity. Times will not be easy, but those of you who can attune to the incoming vibrations should infuse them with love and compassion for your fellows."

"Stones, crystals, trees, flowers, shrubs and all plants enhance the subtle light energies and lovingly blend with them. Remember, certain aspects of these energies wax and wane, just as your own will do on your individual quests."

"Most subtle energy operates in spirals. It can also be present in solid or hollow geometric shapes and can be enhanced, increased or even created anew by such shapes; the location of such constructions and the precise alignment of these are of the very essence of Universal life."

"Treat these re-emerging energies with the greatest respect. There is always the danger of euphoria or over-enthusiasm when one is first exposed to them. This impetuousness, unchecked, can lead to untold complications. If you are fortunate enough to be attuned to the new energies, never misuse or abuse them.'

"Be aware that there are negative energies within the Earth. She has a circulatory system much like the human body and some energy is positive for certain individuals and some is not; what feels negative for one can be positive for another. Like the human bloodstream, the Earth-system has flows of energy with positive and negative polarities, but these can switch from time to time depending upon the time of year, the position of other planets, and so on. Nothing is fixed in finality, all is in motion. It is necessary to 'divine' the flow of each site before ever contemplating working with the energies. Every individual must discover his or her own energy spiral at the time of the intended quest, and then 'divine' the site to be visited; some locations will not suit certain people, and vice versa. Always remember this when working with Earth energies, and never attempt to contain them or hold on to them, for they will surely damage you in the process."

"The human body is a very delicate receiver and transmitter. Never abuse yourself or your body's energies by over-indulgence in anything. Only work with Earth energy when your system is correctly attuned and always remember the stricture about letting it flow through you. Never try to cling to it. No-one could hang onto a shooting star for long, it would surely burn them up! Remember, you are an energy force in your own right. The individual that is YOU in the physical world is a series of vibrations. Even your spoken words have energy. We would ask you to be cautious about certain things you say as they can never be completely forgotten and must be accounted for eventually."

"What you see around you in the material world is composed of different vibrations and it all looks and feels perfectly solid to your senses. Yet, your science tells you that, basically, everything is made up from atoms and molecules which give an impression of solidity. Consequently, everything you see could all be an illusion! Do not be disturbed by this, for there is an elementary law of physics that states: 'Energy cannot be destroyed, merely transformed.' Therefore, as you are an energy force in your own right, it follows that 'You' can never be destroyed; you have no need to fear death, it is simply a transformation of energy."

"What you see in your world is what you have made of it, but consider this; it is the Earth that supplies everything you require for life and living. Within the confines of the Earth herself are all the answers, it is up to you to find the questions that fit them! All these answers are inherently connected with energy; you simply have to attune to them and begin to understand how to formulate the ideas contained therein."

"It has been suggested in your myths that Merlin was imprisoned in a rock or cavern by a young maiden; your tales contain many grains of truth which become distorted by time. Certainly, one particular energy *has* been locked in stone for centuries, but it is about to be 'released'. However, this is only one aspect of the awakening of Merlin!'

'To limit yourself to one aspect of God is a mistake for you severely restrict your perception of the Universe. God is multi-dimensional. In the physical state your sensory apparatus is limited but it is essential for you to realise that God is infinite...'

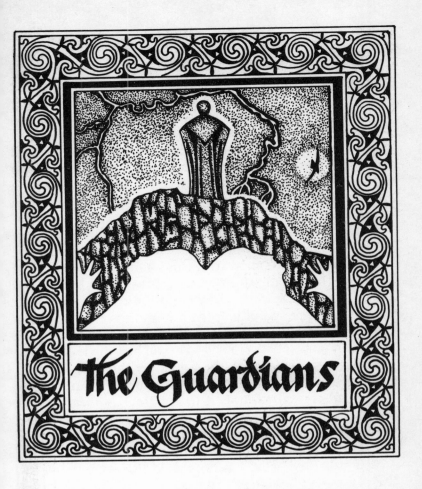

The Guardians

Tangible Sources of Light, Love and Wisdom

Some time after my preliminary meetings with the Mage, he had suggested we should use a code system of recognition between us, in order that I could check the validity of information and communications coming to me from other sources.

He put forward a series of constellation 'call signs' that could be identifiable either directly or through symbolism. There were four in all. If anyone happened to mention one of these, or something easily associated with them, when they wrote or called, I would know that it was a sign from the Mage that they had come to me for a purpose. Conversely, if I needed confirmation of something someone had said and I did not receive the 'call sign' I would be wary of the information until I could verify it in other ways. I found this to be very useful when checking on the bona-fides of particular visitors who professed to be authorities on certain esoteric subjects; the code system has proved its worth on countless occasions.

Since those early days, it has emerged that the Mage selected the constellations most carefully. Ultimately, he stopped using their official titles and started calling three of them the 'Magician'; the 'King'; and the 'Holy Lady'. This emphasis on the stars drew my attention to the heavens far more. Over a period of months it began to dawn on me in 1976 that the Merlin energy was somehow linked with the 'Magician' constellation itself. The night I made this connection, I was standing in the garden; as the truth dawned, a cluster of shooting stars broke from the centre of the 'Magician' constellation as if to confirm my idea. Finally, the import of this message began to sink in and I realised that I was talking with an energy that had its origins, not on the planet Earth, but way out across the Universe!

Was this God? Had I been visited like some latter-day Old Testament prophet? The energy had indicated that names could be misleading, so was 'Merlin' in fact some facet of 'HIM'? I was quickly disabused about the exclusive masculinity of the Ultimate in a subsequent interview.

Q: " 'M', are you God?"

M: "We are *all* part of the Godhead."

Q: "But you seem to fit all the Biblical descriptions of 'Him'."

M: "God is not a 'Him', nor a 'Her' either for that matter! You must try and get away from the restrictions of the material human form. If you were an intelligent rock your concept of God would be visually different, but it is the *same* God, for God is everywhere and in everything. God is a cosmic concept; God is the Universe; God simply *is* . . . "

Q: "Is this why there are so many different Gods in human culture then?"

M: "Of course. Mankind continually strives to explain the inexplicable; define the indefinable. Monotheism is all very well but it never takes into account the changing Cosmic Seasons. The Greeks picked up some very sensible ideas about the Heavens, using allegorical figures to explain particular energies and their effects. But the human images they chose, eventually became all-important to them, and the original energies they were supposed to represent were forgotten.'

Q: "Are you the only Cosmic energy then?"

M: "Good heavens! No! You will find in old Chinese philosophy an indication of the energies present in the ever-changing cosmos. There are a number of energies playing upon the Earth in particular, and each influences your periods of history in turn. But nothing ever remains fixed, that is the Cosmic Law . . . "

Q: "Will I ever meet these other energies?"

M: "Of course!"

*   *   *

True to his word, from late 1976 Merlin went on to introduce me first to the Cosmic 'King' energy and then to the Universal 'Holy Lady'. They were incredible experiences and took place outdoors on clear nights when there was no moonlight to dim the stars. I soon discovered that each of these energies had a connection with a particular area of the heavens. The Mage would ask me to concentrate upon one area of sky and I soon became aware of waves of energy radiating down from the specific constellation involved. Subsequently, I have come to call the three energies 'The

Guardians'. In some strange way, they seem to 'hold court' in the northern sky where their subtle vibrations are forever present and playing upon us. Their intensity appears to vary, in a seasonal sense, for any one of the three can predominate for a time, and then another takes over and the influence subtly changes.

When I first met the 'King' energy, it manifested around me as brilliant blue light that lit up the garden for hundreds of feet in all directions. And yet there was a definite personality associated with it which I found extremely daunting. It was austere, strong and serious; given to action rather than words if the light display was anything to go by! I have since realised that it is a particularly vigorous energy, seeming to be powerful in a 'physical-fitness' way – echoing the Appollonian ideal of perfection, I suppose. 'He' rarely speaks to me other than in clipped, efficient tones, pitched rather low.

I do not feel as much at home with this energy as I do with the magician, for I feel he regards me as a bit of a physical mess! Although, to be fair, like all the energies, the 'King' exudes a tremendous vibration of love – far greater than anything physical.

He seems to epitomise all the gallant heroes one has ever read about. His prowess and strength are unquestionable, and I feel, poor specimen that I am, stirred to assist him in his endless quest.

The 'Holy Lady', on the other hand, has a gentle, beautiful and awe-inspiring presence. Regrettably, she never lingers for very long. I have seen her as an intensely bright golden-pink light. Her 'voice' sounds like high-pitched tinkling bells that leave a resonance in my ears long after she has gone. When she manifests, ground mists foregather like a gentle, soothing mantle of peace. She makes her influence felt in subtle, delicate ways; usually her hand can be seen at work in plants and the landscape. Also, it is *her* heartbreak that one feels when thoughtless actions pollute or decimate the environment. Of the three energies, the Lady seems to affect

me in such a deeply emotional way that it is almost impossible to find precise words to describe the experience.

More recently, the Mage has introduced me to a fourth
energy that corresponds with the original fourth constellation. This colour is a brilliant green and the energy itself
seems to contain elements within it of all the others.
However, I will describe the effects of the fourth energy in
more detail in a later chapter, as it took me long enough to
come to grips with the existence of the original trinity of
Guardians.

*   *   *

Given such mind-boggling concepts as these, I had to have
some kind of independent proof that the Mage was not
merely pulling my leg and that I was not going off my
rocker! I needed some definite philosophical confirmation
for the possible existence of such energies. So I asked the
Magician to suggest a specific source of proof where confir-
matory evidence would be forthcoming. I wanted to check
the plausibility of the cosmic origins of the energies I had
experienced. He simply told me to consult an oracle! Re-
membering his remark about China, I turned to the only
oracle I possessed at the time – the *I-Ching*. There, to my
amazement, I found an 'echo' of the three energies I had
met and conversed with; for the ancient Chinese believed
in such cosmic energies and considered that they played a
vital part in their everyday lives.

The Great Treatise of the *I-Ching* speaks at some length
about three dominant energy influences called the 'trinity
of world principles':

a) the Earth (receptive/feminine);
b) Man (physical);
c) Heaven (creative).

In consequence, I have come to associate the Earth as

being under the aegis of the Holy Lady, the King energy as being directly connected with Mankind, and the wisdom of the Magician with Heaven. What incredible evidence! However, more was to come.

Some years ago, T.C. Lethbridge discovered three prehistoric figures carved in the chalk near the remains of a hill fort at Wandlebury in Cambridgeshire: they were a King, a Lady and a cloaked figure! This trinity of chalk figures echoes the creative energies described in the *I-Ching* in which, to achieve harmony and balance in the world, two male sources combine with one female source.

Guy Underwood, in *Pattern of the Past*, cites three telluric currents of energy that exist within the Earth which often determine the layout of ancient sites – two positive and one negative! What greater confirmation could one ask for?

From the beginning, it seems Merlin deliberately used imagery that could develop as my knowledge and experience grew. The sword, for example, is a symbol I now associate very much with the King; the chalice represents the receptivity of the Holy Lady; and the wand is regarded as the emblem of the Magician. Of course, these three symbols are suits in the Tarot pack, the fourth being coins or pentacles which could represent the cosmic energy that unites all three: yet another connection with the Guardians.

*   *   *

I have only just begun to understand how much these three energies permeate our everyday lives. A good example of the King's influence is the impact that the legends of religious heroes like Jesus, Buddha, Zoroaster, Mohammed, Krishna – and, of course, King Arthur – have all had on human consciousness.

Another essence of all three Guardians can be found in works of fiction by such authors as J.R.R. Tolkien, Mary Stewart, C.S. Lewis and Marion Bradley.

A third is the global success of films like *Star Wars* and *Superman*, whose archetypal heroes wear different garb but embody almost identical themes. Even the structure of certain languages seems to echo the three energies, e.g. 'he', 'she' and 'it'.

I realise it may be difficult enough for the reader to grasp the concept of the existence of *one* cosmic energy, and yet here I am introducing a further two sources of inspiration and enlightenment. *But that is the way it happened.* The Mage, after a couple of years of instruction, blew away any restrictions or restraints that I might have mentally imposed upon our association. By introducing me to the King energy, the Mage helped me to begin to understand what drives and motivates the 'hero' figures of our history and why we need them. Similarly, I began to appreciate the Holy Lady's influence through the Moon, the seasons, the Earth Mother, her craft worshippers and her matriarchs of the past too. But like the Greeks before me I discovered the only way I could begin to comprehend and define the energies was by investing them with personalities. I was obliged to anthropomorphize them, for my limited sensory apparatus insisted upon it! However, I soon observed that their moods subtly changed with the passage of the months and the progression of the seasons, each energy having at least three different phases, or faces. This helped me to grasp why certain religions embrace polytheistic concepts of God, like the triple Goddess in ancient Greece, or the Roman God Janus who had at least two faces. I felt I was beginning to touch some of the keys to the very mysteries of existence that are only ever hinted at in esoteric literature.

Whether or not we are students or explorers of such mysteries, we all now stand at the dawn of the Age of Aquarius. It is reputedly a time of change. The symbol for Aquarius has been been personified by a figure pouring water from a vessel, or even a phoenix rising from the flames. But what do these symbols mean?

The Age of Pisces (fishes) is behind us and the age of Aquarius (rebirth) is just ahead. Of course, the precession of the equinoxes, a total of 26,000 years, dictates the area of sky through which the sun travels, in relation to the Earth, across 12 or 13 periods of approximately 2,000 – 2,160 years; each aeon being given the constellation or zodiacal sign corresponding with that particular area of sky. The Sun is now fast approaching Aquarius. But as I have begun to see, the Guardian energies permeate our very existence, do they perhaps influence each age as well, giving rise to matriarchal or patriarchal ideologies?

Could the pendulum of the cosmic clock be swinging from one Guardian influence to another, thus lending a certain emphasis to each age in turn? Certainly, the present patriarchal hero system has outlived its long tenure and looks a little jaded today. Are we now entering an age that could strike a balance between matriarchy and patriarchy? An age of forebearance and wisdom? Will the phoenix usher in another Golden Age – perhaps the Age of the Magician?

I, for one, profoundly hope so; but this cannot simply be achieved by leaving it all to the Guardians. WE have to help to bring such ideals into manifestation. Characteristically, the Mage has given us a plethora of advice on this subject, although he insists these are not dogmatic instructions, merely suggestions.

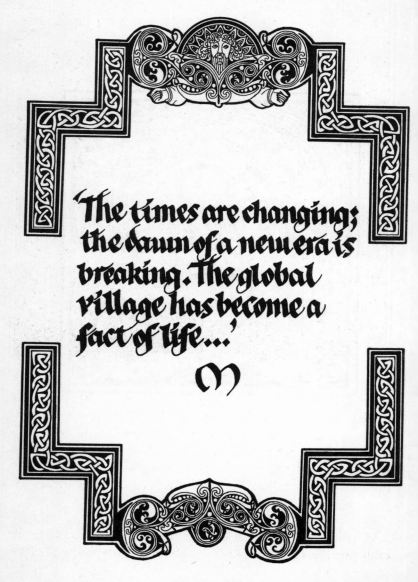

'The times are changing;
the dawn of a new era is
breaking. The global
village has become a
fact of life...'

M

Rhapsody of Hope

How does one prepare to meet a New Age? Will it strike swiftly? Will its onset be gradual? The Mage has often referred to a coming time of upheaval and how best to cope with it. I have, therefore, grouped together a selection of his suggestions related to self-improvement and social awareness. I hope they help you in the troubled times ahead.

*   *   *

"As you all prepare to enter another Age, vibrant new energies are replacing the old. Some long-dormant energies, too, are being given a new lease of life. One of these is a positive feminine element manifesting in womankind. For far too long, man has dominated his women; bent them to his every whim and caprice; degraded them and made them his bond-slaves. The reign of the patriarch is ending – his going will not be pleasant. However, womankind would do well to remember that this time a pendulum swing from patriarchy to matriarchy must not recur. Let every woman see, in the new-found enthusiasm that surrounds her as she glimpses freedom, that she and her sisters must have the wisdom and compassion to accept that what we are seeking is a balance; mutual respect and interdependence between the sexes. This will take the special kind of selflessness woman possesses. She will have to re-educate her man in sensitivity. Wisdom, truth, trust, honesty, forgiveness and love must prevail – not revenge!"

"Mankind will not be permitted to ride roughshod into the Universe. He will simply find himself accepted when he finds HIMSELF – his true self that is at one with the rest of us!"

"Sensitivity is a double-edged sword, for it opens up channels of every kind. Be sure that, as your sensitivity grows, you develop a sense of discrimination."

"Every person has the potential to attain the power to bring about change, although not all manage to achieve this. If you believe that you have uncovered a profound Truth which could enhance the destiny of mankind – and you are pure in heart and mind, pursuing unselfish motives – then it is your duty to tell the world. Whether the world will listen is another matter!"

"It is vitally important that you learn how to undertake a positive 'spring-cleaning' of the spirit, it affects your continued physical well-being. This is accomplished through diet and meditation. Try and avoid, if possible, processed food contaminated with chemicals for such additives 'fight' each other inside your body! Natural foodstuffs are the healthiest things to eat. Try growing your own or, if your circumstances make this difficult, demand uncontaminated food from your supplier; fresh wholesome food free of poisonous chemical additives. You should be able to apply financial pressure to food manufacturers by boycotting unhealthy foodstuffs."

"Do be more aware of your diet. Increasingly, chemicals are being introduced into the food chain; some of them induce stomach complaints, and others allergic reactions. Be careful of your drinking water too, for over-farming methods are polluting water supplies with chemicals at an alarming rate. Consider your food purchases most carefully, your continued good health depends upon it. Try and achieve a sensible balance in your eating habits and remember that unscrupulous manufacturers are looking for profits, they are not safe-guarding your health."

"Too many of you in affluent nations rely upon your local supermarket to supply all your needs, with no thought to the methods of production. You have abnegated the responsibility for growing your foodstuffs onto someone else, and in the process have lost touch with the source that supplies your every requirement. This is producing a breed of highly selfish men and women who scream with indignation at the first sign of shortages, with no thought to the causes. Are you such a person? Show respect for the planet that nurtures you; say a personal 'thank you' by planting the occasional tree or shrub of your own; or by replenishing the Earth in some other way."

"If you all practised a little restraint, or self-denial each day, vast acreages of forest and countryside could be preserved; huge areas of ocean and rivers would be protected. In consequence, a whole spectrum of life-forms could be allowed to continue living, as their habitat would be preserved. Think about it! As long as you all continue to consume resources without any sense of responsibility you will undermine the very life-support system that sustains you."

45

"Devise whatever methods you can to recycle waste products. Look at the mountains of garbage and food waste that accumulate each day in major cities; this often spills out into the surrounding countryside. Valiant efforts are made to clear it away and yet back it all comes again in a fresh accumulation. Remember, the resources of the Earth are not limitless."

"Let your children blossom like flowers. Give them strength and understanding. Encourage their growth in a mindful way. Remember, to produce healthy plants it is sometimes necessary to restrict wild growth, so with your children – but use discipline wisely."

"Your world is one enormous classroom to which you return time and time again, until you have learned all the lessons that Life has to offer."

"Weigh carefully the advisability of joining a cult of any kind. You can best serve yourself and the coming age by thinking for yourself and encouraging others to do likewise. Cults, secret societies, even fanatical governments crush individuality, actively discourage you from personal responsibility and invariably lead to élitism – or worse!"

"Evil is the product of selfish human acts, not of 'fallen angels'. There are no 'forces of evil' in the inner realms waging perpetual war with 'forces of light'. It is your own higher self that places the occasional obstacles and hardships in your path – for very positive reasons. The 'seven planes', as so often described, are merely different levels of confusion and wish-fulfilment – the astral planes. Infinite realms of Spirit lie beyond; never forget how limited the 'seven levels' are and how they have kept mankind locked in the here-below. Look beyond these thought planes to your real source. *We all come from it!*"

"I realise that many of you feel that you are prisoners in a financial treadmill that denies you the freedom to live your life without harmful strain and stress. But think! – you will remain 'caught' in this mire until you decide to get out of it.

The only one who can make the decision to move is you."

"Your physical life is for living; explore it to the full. Life is the gift of high and low alike; never coerce others into action, particularly if you are fortunate enough to be in a position of authority over them."

"For too long the weak have been oppressed and down-trodden by those in power; a great trust has been abused. Instead of using the opportunities to exercise compassion powermongers have gloated over those in less favourable positions. Those who have corrupted the system will pay the price for what they have created. Always ensure that your intentions are honest, caring and truthful in your deal-ings with others."

"Within each one of you lies a divine spark, a divine light. Many of you obscure that light by moving away from it; or lose sight of it. Only through right action and inten-tion can you increase your personal light intensity."

"Those who are lost in darkness have created a void within and around themselves; their light still burns but it is hidden deep inside and obscured by darkness of their own making. It takes a very special energy indeed to be able to reach into that darkness and illuminate it from outside."

"In the past, those in power have had to use torture, inquisition and even death to enforce their authority, for they realised that the very citadel of their power was built upon the sands of treachery, falsehood and the suppression of Truth; if this was not the case there would be no need to enforce their rule. Truth shines in its own light. You should ensure your future works avoid such terrible mistakes by keeping to what you know is Truth and never placing too much dominance into the hands of one person or social group. You must take a collective responsibility for the care of yourselves, your fellows and your planet."

"I wish it were possible to show you some of the subtler beauties of the inner worlds, and for you to enjoy the tran-scendent experiences this entails. This must wait until your perceptions are more refined. All I can offer you is an occasional glimpse of colour in the natural world around you that hints at what lies beyond."

"It is for all of you to prove yourselves worthy of removing the 'veils' that surround you. Until you can put aside arrogance and the need to dominate others or have power over them, you will never achieve the true sight. There is no enemy other than the one within you. Learn self-control and you will begin to find peace and true vision."

"You are all returning to the great Light as day follows day, but it is incumbent upon you to try and achieve a greater degree of inner illumination so that your reunion with the Divine will be truly blessed."

"Open your hearts and your minds to the pulse of the coming age, and you will reap greater rewards than you could ever imagine."

'Look upward, many clues lie in the stars. Are not stars hidden in the day when the life-giving rays of the Sun are at work? Yet energies from constellations are far more subtle. Night time is the period for true contemplation, to seek spiritual enlightenment. The stars are in specific places and point the way to the answers of the story you seek. But if you ask for a sign, be patient enough to wait for it ...'

The Master of Ceremonies

In 1981, the fourth energy emerged – the strangest of all to understand or fully comprehend. At first, I thought of it as a synthesis of the three prime energies, but events have proved otherwise. The fourth figure to introduce itself has been what I call the Priest/Mystic. Whilst at college, I devoted my dissertation to this Dionysian-type of wild energy that seems to be the complement of the Kingly element of order. This, the fourth energy, is quite as important as the other three, although its major influence is only really apparent for a quarter of the year. It could be said to epitomise the true 'Priest' figure, the Master of Mysteries, Leader of the Dance, the Conductor of all pageant, ritual and ceremony.

*   *   *

The Greek figure traditionally associated with this type of energy is Dionysus, the so-called God of Disorder. This is a misnomer. The Dionysian energy is a vital and integral part of human nature; as are, I believe, the other three. To ignore any of these energies is to deny a part of ourselves; but to ignore the fourth is to invite real problems.

The human spirit has a need to break away from the restrictions of the twentieth century lifestyle. Who has not felt the urge to go barefoot in the grass, to try nude bathing, or to leave the rat-race, if only for a few days or even hours, and run free? This fourth energy calls to us, offering the pursuit of happiness and abandon. To ignore such calls is to build frustration; to create problems that might eventually require therapy of one sort or another to put right. Conversely, to embrace this energy alone and ignore the balancing effects of the other three is equally dangerous. The eventual downfall of that great magus Aleister Crowley is a prime example of how 'do what thou wilt' cannot possibly be 'the whole of the Law'.

The Greeks believed that their gods did not expect worship, in the sense we understand it today, but simply an acknowledgement of their existence and ever-presence. Given the increasing psychological and psychiatric problems of our society, perhaps we should follow their example?

The Mystic energy I feel is the well-spring of the creator, the artist, the inventor, the dancer, the actor, even the blacksmith. Anything related to the physical arts comes under the sway of this energy. It is what promotes innovation and change; it prevents anything going stale. How dull is the world for those who ignore the call of *this* creative force!

In the quartet of the Guardians we now observe two types of leader figure – the King and his opposite number the Mystic/Priest (Arthur and Lancelot perhaps?). In the Hellenistic pantheon, Apollo was the Kingly symbol of order, beauty and strength, healing, music, poetry, archery and prophecy – the conscious mind. Dionysus was the symbol of our instinctive side – the subconscious. This wild energy has been feared and mistrusted by all forms of authority down through the ages, although it is not naturally destructive in itself. The King and the Mystic are therefore like twins, or two sides of a coin, for one polarity cannot exist without the other. I suggest we could be looking here at archetypes of our physical and spiritual natures. Ironically, it seems, from my researches, that the King figure is linked to the physical world, concerned with the maintenance of order, whereas the Mystic is of the spiritual and change. This could help to explain why a strict imposition of order on spiritual matters produces such negative results and reactions!

Here is a very curious piece of information: in Greek mythology Apollo was reputed to go North for three or four months of the year to feast and carouse with the Hyperboreans during the winter. It is as though he took on the opposite rôle of his twin, or brother. Therefore, it is somewhat staggering to discover that the constellation associated with the fourth energy, which Merlin indicated to me, does only appear in the northern night skies during the course of the autumn and winter!

Incredibly, the Great Treatise of the *I-Ching* also talks of a system of order and disorder being the 'Third nexus of events in the world'. Given that Heaven (Mage) and Earth (Holy Lady) are the other two energies involved, then the third seems to be split into a duality of opposites – the King and the Mystic, presumably? The Chinese believed that the three basic energies primarily showed their influence in the world through Men (King), Animals (Magician) and Plants (Holy Lady). The fourth element worked through 'Chance' and was, therefore, closely allied with Man, wherein lies the basic influence of the King.

Between them, I believe the four Guardian energies have inspired mythological archetypes in *all* cultures; like Adam and Eve with their two sons Cain and Abel, for example. The constellations that I was originally given, and that have subsequently become points of focus for me when contemplating these energies are as follows:

THE KING The first constellation given was Draco (the Dragon); this was later extended to include Hercules – the archetypal hero who undertook the twelve labours. Coincidentally, the constellation of Hercules is positioned at the tail end of the solar/zodiacal year, on my astronomical planisphere (a normal, commercially available item), as though contemplating the full extent of all the other signs. This figure has all the trappings of a King around it in the night sky. There is the Northern Crown; the Lyre; the Eagle; the power to handle serpents – Ophiuchus (healing); and the Dragon – a symbol of Earth energy. The constellations of Scorpio and Sagittarius lie close by and could be associated with this Kingly archetype.

THE HOLY LADY This beautiful energy was identified by the constellation Cassiopeia. The configuration portrays a

Queen with her arms upraised in benediction. Around her are grouped the winged horse Pegasus; Cygnus – the swan; Perseus, the legendary slayer of the Medusa; and Andromeda – the daughter of Cassiopeia. The constellations of Pisces and Aquarius seem to be connected with her.

THE MAGICIAN   The first energy to manifest to me used as its primary call sign the constellation Ursa Major – the Great Bear. This is Merlin's realm in the night sky. Behind him lie two lions – large and small; to one side the ploughman or Bear-Keeper; around him the hunting-dogs; the Sextant; the Sickle; the Tresses of Princess Berenice; the Crow and the Cup. Merlin's closest ecliptical constellations are Leo and Virgo.

THE MYSTIC   Associated with the constellation of Orion, this energy has around it in the skies the Hare; the two dogs Canis Major and Minor (including the 'Dog Star' Sirius); the Bull; the Pleiades; and Eridanus the river. Before him lies the charioteer – Auriga, and the twins – Castor and Pollux. To one side lies the Unicorn. The associated constellations of the ecliptic are Gemini and Taurus. Orion appears in the southern part of the northern night skies for part of the autumn and winter, dropping below the horizon during the spring and summer.

Originally, the figure of the Mystic (Orion) may have been thought to vanish from the northern heavens each year, disappearing into the Earth, the sea or the river, to be reborn after the autumnal equinox. Robert Temple, in his book *The Sirius Mystery*, explains the ancient obsession with the heliacal rising of particular stars and constellations, as being connected with certain energies that ebbed and flowed. Personally, I have found the autumn to be a period of the year when psychic and spiritual energy reaches a peak, which steadily declines after Christmas. The autumnal equinox seems to mark the overture of this gradual increase in supernatural energy.

Undoubtedly, a great many of the star alignments associated with stone circles in the northern hemisphere must have been studied and constructed during the long dark nights of winter and in a period when the climate was more conducive to such activities! It is worth noting also that during the Mediaeval period the 'Festival of Fools' ran from early November to early February. This was a time when masters would wait upon servants, the whole world organisation could be stood on its head, and any man could be King-for-a-day. Indeed, this surrogate 'King' was often ritually 'sacrificed' or de-throned to promote continued well-being and fertility, thus ensuring that the real King could be safely 're-born' after the festivities! In the ancient Middle East, the Akkadians and the Sumerians had many such death and rebirth scenarios in their canon of beliefs, involving heroes (or gods) who descended into the sea or the bowels of the Earth. Small wonder that their descendants, the Hebrews, 'borrowed' their cosmologies from these beliefs. Even today, this period of the year is associated with the birth of the Christian saviour/ superhero, who died and was born again. The death and resurrection story is an old and much-used one.

Over the centuries the autumn and winter have been associated with feasting and drinking as well. The Bacchanalian and Saturnalian festivals occurred during this time of the year reaching a peak at the moment of the winter solstice when the light is 're-born'. Interestingly, at midnight on the day of the winter solstice, the four Guardian constellations are arranged in the northern sky at the four cardinal points of the compass!

Could some ancient mythology be a fanciful way of describing the movement of important constellations across the night sky? I feel certain that the four major constellations do have a strong effect upon us from my own acquaintance with their various manifestations. The Chinese studied cosmic energy and the stars for many thousands of years and their various philosophies, like Taoism, seem to indicate they had knowledge of the four basic energy arch-etypes I have mentioned. In fact, the *I-Ching* describes a 'cosmic family' of *eight* trigrams (or energies) that appear to be dualities of the four primary Guardian figures set in a circle. The whole configuration is like a wheel. The constellations too are set around the heavens describing a circle overhead. Perhaps it is symbolic of the transmigration of souls? The wheel of rebirth? Karma.

'A belief in the laws of
Karma and the wheel
of rebirth is returning
to the West – this
knowledge should never
have left!'   M

Karma

In this collection of his sayings, the Magician begins to outline the workings of the laws of consequence and how our present existence is governed by past actions and previous lives. He explains how our attitude towards things around us creates the very world we inhabit; how we can be our own worst enemy or our own best friend. From his comments, it is interesting to note that we must have been fully aware of these laws at one time, but somehow we seem to have forgotten them!

"Consider the following: what is meant by 'as you sow – so shall you reap'? Just this, your every thought, word and action not only reverberates throughout the world but even affects realms beyond. Little do you realise what havoc your selfishness creates in the delicate balance of things. Enlarge your perspective, learn to develop a sense of responsibility for everything you undertake."

"You must all strive to take more care in your decision-making. Thoughtless actions can cost lives."

"As humanity approaches the millennium, instant karma is becoming one means to redress many injustices – especially those perpetuated by men who are ignorant of the Universal law and refuse to acknowledge the growing spiritual awareness all around them."

"Make no mistake, great wrongs have been done, and a price will have to be paid. But no one man can absolve the whole of humanity from individual responsibility."

"Remember, no-one will judge your life but yourself. This you will do when your present incarnation ends, in the 'light of all-knowing'. Do not expect perfection in the material world for it will always elude you."

"You are all at different stages of development, so equality is just not possible. And so I say to those of you in positions of power over your fellows – be doubly sure that you do not abuse this privilege, lest your short-sightedness set up repercussions that will hound you for lifetimes."

"Do not be unduly distressed if negativity appears to be reaching a triumphant peak in your life – it shall not prevail! The wheel of life, and fortune continually revolves; everything is subject to change. Like the Tao of the old philosophers, the great river of Time flows onward, sweeping away all futile efforts to divert or block its path. Time is possibly the greatest healer."

"Do not castigate yourself if you make mistakes. No-one is perfect. Balance is what you truly seek. Look beyond your outer personality for the *real* you within; once you have found it, try and attune your outer personality to this innermost being."

"Remember, material science does *not* hold all the answers; there is always room for both commonsense and intuition. This is why your brain has a left and a right hemisphere! Avoid a mechanistic way of thinking, for there are often better and more natural ways of achieving your ends. The ancients understood this balancing process and attempted to incorporate it into their everyday lives, just as you should."

"Let your inner emotions and feelings tell you what feels 'right'. Throw out anything that does not harmonise, until you can reach to the very heart of the matter. The solutions are almost always *within you*."

"Snap judgements are made in your world that often have far-reaching consequences for generations to come. Remember, this can *never* be the way of the Spirit, for great thought and deliberation should attend all such undertakings."

"Never ignore your physical 'vehicle', or its needs; they are a determining factor in your daily life. One of the prime functions of your lives on Earth is to allow your spiritual nature to evolve. We cannot do it for you. We can advise, but not interfere; we can sweep away some of the mental debris that surrounds you, most of which you have put there yourself(!); we can point the way to higher paths; *but we cannot walk them for you*. We can open your eyes, to a degree, but no further – the rest is up to you. What you make of your lives and your world is your own responsibility."

"Some of your companions in the physical world think they know all the answers; the dangerous ones try and *impose* their solutions upon the rest."

"Do not fall into the trap of thinking that mankind is all-important; for mankind is but one small cog in a wheel, of a gigantic machine called life."

"Ask yourself why it should be necessary for men to be forever creating invisible or exterior adversaries? It is because they haven't the courage to face the one inside!'

"There are no demons or devils – only excuses! Such creations were introduced by religious 'authorities', from the pagan shaman to the churchmen of the Middle-ages, to enslave free-thinking peoples through fear and superstition. Remember, that certain physical men are still only a step or two removed from savagery. What do you think happened to the souls of the dinosaurs? Some people can behave savagely with very little provocation, but evil is not a case of external forces playing about with the destiny of mankind – it is an aspect of himself! Until man learns to face himself, to think clearly and accept responsibility for everything he undertakes, the swing from intelligence to barbarism will continue."

"It is the situation in which you find yourself and how you deal with it, that makes you what you are. By now you will have discerned that negative experiences teach you far more than positive."

"Do not be too harsh on those who cannot walk your path, for they cannot see as you do or even feel as you do. It is not easy for anyone to be truly objective."

"Stir others into action when they come to you for advice, otherwise they will sit back and let you do all the work, and then criticise your efforts, for the human animal is by nature a lazy creature! But such is not to be the way of the coming age. Each must *do* – not wait for it to be done for them. Your senses have been dulled by too much easy living. Instead of sitting around fuming at the destruction of your environment do something about it! Instead of climbing the walls, start building some – or at least some foundations for the future."

"Never forget how limited is the understanding of the majority when it comes to international or cosmic concepts that affect the lives of millions.

"In the physical body you cannot reach the higher realms; you are far too dense (in more ways than one!), but higher beings can descend the ladder of vibration to assist you in times of direst need. Nor can you hope to grasp all the complexities of the Great Plan in the restricted form of the material body. Anyone who claims to know all the answers when in a physical vehicle is sadly mistaken. By all means follow the path of inner wisdom, and achieve a degree of balance so that you can attune to a higher pitch of understanding. But you are limited. Although you can still achieve great things if you follow the impulses of light and love."

"Violent, destructive action does not solve anything, except to create further karmic debts; it is a temporary aberration, usually created through fear or ignorance. Why should there be a need for any man to dominate another? Until you can throw away such arrogance, this craving for power over others, you will never achieve true understanding; the doors leading to the higher realms will remain firmly closed. Purity, of intention and motivation, is the key to unlock them."

"Try and attune yourself to the rhythm of the Cosmos, do not fight against it. Let us help you begin to help yourself."

"Consider this – many people see only what they wish to see ignoring the unacceptable or the unpalatable. It is no use averting your eyes from the distasteful, for it is just as much your responsibility, if you do nothing to put it right, as that of the person who created it."

"If you seek honestly for the Truth, the love and the balance that make up the Great Plan, you will find that you already possess the inner strength and wisdom to survive the coming changes. Do not struggle blindly against the negative influences in the world around you, lest you become part of them. Gentle persuasion and example are the keys to coping with adverse situations. Make active effort within and be more positive without; become tolerant of those who cannot understand as you do and show compassion towards those who cause you suffering, for one day they will realise the result of their actions; if you really care about your world and your fellows then the darkness will fall away from you as if it had never existed, and you will shine with pure light."

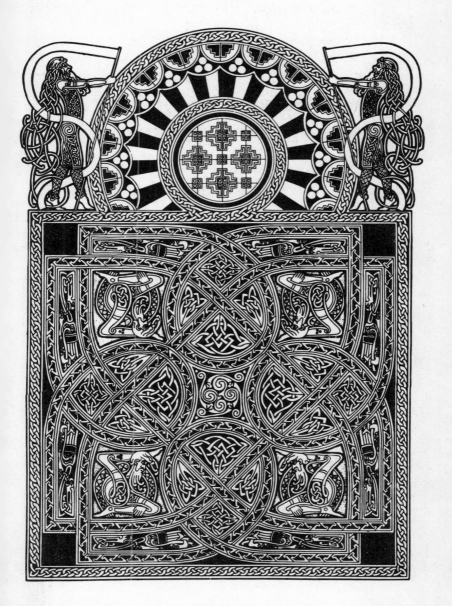

'Try to regard your life as a milestone, or a signpost along the path. Endeavour to make what is written upon you clear, in order that those who follow a similar path may benefit from your experience...'

M

Beacons of Light Milestones

In order to introduce the four Cosmic Energies it was necessary, in a previous chapter, to jump forward a number of years to 1981 when the Master of Ceremonies first appeared. However, the intervening years were equally filled with mystical visions, 'coincidences', revelations and magic. Some had more impact on me than others, for in each case I was looking for the more familiar evidence of the Magician's influence, rather than the other three energies.

During the intervening period, I was undergoing a kind of spiritual metamorphosis. As I explained, prior to the appearance of the Merlin energy, my life had been commercially oriented. I had given no time to spiritual matters since my youth. My energies were devoted entirely to the pursuit of fame and fortune. Basically, this was due to a disillusionment with established religion, and a devotion to the twentieth century version of the God of Mammon! But the Messianic appearance of the Merlin energy in my bedroom brought about a spiritual catharsis.

I am told that my whole personality began to change – for the better, I might add. Subsequently, my time was given over to periods of extensive study. I sought for, and found, confirmation of Merlin's existence in a variety of different places and different ideologies. To this end, I first visited the famed ancient site of Stonehenge in 1975, but did not *seem* to pick up any apparent connections with Merlin at the time. However, the monument itself proved to be another spiritual catalyst to me, despite my not sensing the physical 'presence' of the energy I had expected.

Having found no sensory impression of Merlin on the first visit to Stonehenge, I decided to go again with my wife on Midsummer Eve. Imagine our horror to discover that Stonehenge resembled a First World War battlefield, with coils of barbed wire positioned so as to prevent access to the stones. Only a handful of modern Druids – practioneers of the nineteenth century innovation – were allowed inside the circle, watched from outside by a hundred or so spectators. The atmosphere did not appear conducive to good vibrations; many visitors were disgruntled by the presence of the barbed wire.

I felt that we were, perhaps, on a 'fool's errand'. However, I reckoned without the Magician's potent empathy with the animal kingdom and the effect of the waking sun. As the sky began to show the faintest glimmer of light, first one, then three, then *hundreds* of larks rose from the surrounding plain in a tumultuous song of joy. It was a sound which must have lifted the hearts of all those present, as it did ours. Unlike the majority of the audience, whose attention was focused on the position of the rising sun, we were looking at the stones themselves. Suddenly, in the half-light, we understood why Stonehenge is known as the 'Giant's Dance'; for we could swear that the stones were oscillating from side to side as if they were dancing.

We left the site before the sun had fully risen, as we felt that we had witnessed the important part of the event most relevant to us.

*   *   *

The Magician has a wonderful sense of fun. Examples of this can be seen in the incredible games he plays during our geomantic excursions. We sometimes get hopelessly lost and have to be 'rescued' by animals or birds that have obviously been sent to guide us; we see laughing faces in cloud formations that appear just at the time we see the funny side of a situation, then vanish in seconds; symbols leap out of the surrounding landscape when we finally discover the correct route, and we see his name or constellation written on road signs, pub signs, lorries, garages, hoardings – even in shop windows.

All this may sound like coincidence, but the timing involved has to be experienced first hand in order to appreciate just how it convinces us that he is ever-present. For example, one truly remarkable incident occurred in 1979 on our way home from a visit to the Malvern Hills. Such expeditions are always filled with hilarity and raucous laughter, and it was during a crazy interlude travelling along the motorway that a friend of ours, in truly flamboyant style, announced: "The answer to the riddle of the Universe will be written on the number plates of a blue and a red car!"

From that moment on, until we reached London, we did not see a single intelligible number plate, or a blue or red car! Having dropped our friends off in London, we headed for home in Hertfordshire. We were waiting at a major road intersection when an *enormous* blue sports car overtook us, closely followed by an even larger red sports car. The combined noise of their exhausts would have captured the attention of the partially deaf! The letters on the number plate of the first car were M E R, and the second L Y N. We felt we had indeed been given one of the answers to the riddle of the Universe, and given it by an energy with a wicked sense of humour that had made us wait over two hours for that answer!

There have been many such incidents over the years and to detail everything would take far too long. Therefore, in deference to the Mage's advice at the head of this chapter, I have selected what I consider to be the most informative material that could prove of some use to others.

Following the period 1975–76, I underwent for the next two years an intensive spiritual re-education. Four incidents from that whole period stand out like beacons of light. They left deep and lasting impressions on me and I have come to regard them as four 'milestones' along my personal pathway of awareness. Each milestone is fronted with a pertinent comment from the Mage.

'How often have you heard it said that the most profound answers are often the simplest ones?'

M

Milestone One
The Quest
Begins

Almost immediately after the first manifestation of the Merlin energy in 1975, I began a spiritual and geomantic quest. Under the oak tree in our garden lengthy teaching sessions took place with the Magician which started me on a new life cycle. From the moment I accepted Merlin's presence in my life, it was as if a major doorway opened in my mind and I saw everything in a totally different light. Indeed, it was as if someone had turned on the light in the darkened room that used to be my consciousness. I realised how much I had been taking for granted.

During this spiritual metamorphosis, I found a growing appreciation within me of natural, tangible energies in the landscape. Becoming aware of earth energy was profoundly moving; it was like waking up to the realisation of how much I had been missing since the innocence of childhood. It is difficult to explain the entire process that occurred to me, but it felt as if the earth energy kept on opening further doorways in my mind, allowing me to become more and more susceptible to natural and supernatural stimulation. I found it easier to accept the notion of a land called 'Faerie' and the magic that surrounds such a domain. Indeed, I understood for the first time what motivates creative people to write inspiring poetry or great music. I suppose I was returning to a more natural state of being; having insulated myself in a 'cocoon of technology' for the whole of my life. Yet, it felt right to be sloughing off my dependence upon twentieth century luxuries if I was ever to begin to understand the Earth and my place upon it.

To be touched by such natural magic is a truly incredible sensation. It was an experience that I found particularly relevant to my personal quest for Truth, for to be truly spiritually aware one has also to be geomantically aware; the two are synonymous. Nevertheless, I would never have learned this lesson without the intercession of the Magician. He sent my whole family out on a geomantic crusade.

It all began with the Mage prompting me to take up long-distance rambling. At first I thought it was to improve my health, but of course that was only part of the plan. I became so adept at walking I sometimes covered as much as ten or fifteen miles at a stretch. In fact, I started to walk everywhere, leaving the car at home. Consequently, the pace of my life altered and I realised just how much of life I had been missing. Rushing around in the course of my film business meant that I had ignored the beauties that Mother Nature paints afresh every day.

The Mage once said to me: "How often have you watched

the sun rise or set? I mean *really* absorbed it? Yet the birds daily celebrate such joyous occasions with song . . . "

I quickly remedied the fault and can say that sunwatching comes highly recommended! Whenever time permits, I still try and watch the day go down.

On my longer walks I noticed how, previously, I had often mooched along with downcast eyes, deep in some financial or emotional turmoil. On my new country rambles, I felt as if I was becoming a living part of the changing cycle of seasons and my eyes were everywhere, trying not to miss anything. I drank in all the stimuli the natural world could offer, often taking my two young daughters along with me. Children are so open to these phenomena and we often stood for hours, just looking around.

Not being a painter, I cannot fully appreciate the technical difficulties involved in setting a landscape on canvas. However, I do admire the expertise that keeps a particular lighting effect in the mind. One does not realise how rapidly the light changes on the landscape until one stops to look. In my opinion, photography comes a poor second to the traditional artist. It seems to me a 'soft' technological option, I suppose, as instant pictures; but both painting and photography have their uses, as I was to find out.

In the summer of 1975, I felt a growing need to visit 'magical' sites. Thus, at the behest of Merlin, my wife and I scheduled trips to Stonehenge, Glastonbury and Avebury, as a beginning. We also sought for further confirmation of the presence of the Mage from sources that my wife trusted within the spiritualist movement – although we did not accept anything blindly.

So it was that we found ourselves, some time later, enjoying an evening in the company of Ivor James who specialises in clairvoyance and psychic artistry, often drawing a person's spirit guide, or mentor, whilst giving the sitter a great deal of evidential information about the connection. Prior to this meeting, we had made a preliminary flying visit to Stonehenge with the children, where I had taken a number of photographs.

Two images to emerge from these seemingly disparate events were interesting to compare as they both showed a bearded man looking from left to right. Ivor James described his drawing thus: "It is someone closely associated with you; I cannot be more specific than that. I'm sorry, this is most unusual . . . "

In contrast, the photograph I took at Stonehenge was a complete 'accident'; I was trying to achieve an effect with the sun emerging around the stone and had paid no attention to the cloud formation in the picture. I was astounded to see outlined in the clouds on the photograph virtually the same bearded figure as the one Ivor James had drawn for me in charcoal!

It is worth explaining here, that unlike the later visit already described, our first trip to the site of Stonehenge had proved deeply moving. We were lucky enough to be allowed to move in amongst the monoliths before they were completely wired off from the general public. I found the stones and their method of construction mind-boggling. Leaving aside the controversy over their actual erection, the sheer logistical problems that must have faced an earlier civilisation are still stupefying to the modern age. The fact that Merlin has been linked with their alleged history came as an additional bonus to me.

Although we were not aware for several weeks of Merlin's face appearing between the upright stones, the image does suggest to me a strong connection between Merlin and Stonehenge. In my photograph, he seems to be looking through the space between the two upright sarsens, reflecting the use of these spaces as lines of sight; and the position of the sun in the photograph, I feel, indicates mental 'illumination' of some kind. Perhaps Merlin was the intellectual genius behind the construction of Stonehenge? He certainly looks to be laughing heartily in the photograph, which is truly characteristic. Obviously, he knows something that we do not!

The photograph was actually processsed about a week *after* the psychic drawing was received, although it had been taken some time *before*. When we compared the two, I found what I consider to be spectacularly convincing evidence for the existence of Merlin; both images fitted my imagined view of the Magician in human guise.

After this period, everything we experienced became linked in some way with the Arthurian mythology of Britain, as if Merlin had chosen this as a focus for our benefit.

'Take comfort: If the Earth were to be destroyed too many other spiritual enterprises would be terminated; therefore it will simply not be allowed to occur...'

ℳ

Milestone two
Visions of Things
to Come

At seven minutes past midnight into the seventh day of the
seventh month of 1977, I was standing alone in a garden in
the shadow of the Malvern Hills. All around me I could
sense the presence of Merlin like an awesome vortex of
energy. I knew that something important was about to
occur; some information was about to be revealed that contained seeds for the future.

Without preamble, the Mage began to expound upon
aspects of the 'Arthurian' energy. He explained that the
series of Arthurian legends, which became known in the

Middle Ages as the 'Matter of Britain', can be shown to have serious relevance without necessarily being taken literally; it is what lies behind the stories that is important. It involves a knowledge of the four Energies, a sense of 'belonging to the Land', and it concerns an harmonious connection reaching back through history – *although we have yet to discover just how far back.*

He also explained how we had to search for the true Round Table of legend, and how the 'Matter of Britain' could affect the future of the whole World. The extraordinary aspect of the whole matter is how the Arthurian legends do indeed seem to find an empathy with people in many different countries, something that I failed to realise at the time.

Much of what he told me then appears elsewhere in this book; but on a personal level, I was given instructions for my own future work.

To be absolutely certain of my ground, I asked for a tangible sign that what I was hearing was correct, and that what I was seeing in vision was Truth. At the very moment that I formed the question in my mind, a shooting star broke from the middle of the constellation I associate with the King, and I saw a sword revealed in awesome brilliance, outlined in the stars of Draco the Dragon. I wept for sheer joy, and bowed my head, for I realised I had just seen Excalibur. The heavens were shimmering with such an intensity that the garden itself was illuminated. It was a breathless moment, which no words are adequate to describe. I felt humbled and insignificant. As I raised my eyes again, I understood that I was witnessing the beginning of the first 'note' in a new Cosmic Overture. As the rippling shimmer of sound and light spread out across the sky another energy joined us adding its blue brilliance to the swirling purple. As I stood transfixed within this intense Arthurian vibration, the voice of the King spoke to me:

"As has long been foretold, an 'Arthur' figure will be back among his people in their time of need, to stimulate them into action – but *this* time we will not do it all for them! 'Knights' and 'Ladies' are gathering in isolated groups, drawn together by some hidden purpose. When the time is right, the principal players will meet at a given place, little known on the physical plane."

"We will appear to them and they will know then what they must do. Their courage must be that of lions, for at that moment there will be no place for the faint-hearted."

"Until the appointed day I say to *all* 'Knights' and 'Ladies' utilise the power wherever you find it; be quite determined in so doing. If we are to succeed you must learn to leap over the heads of amblers and dabblers. Your tasks are to *do*, not just to observe . . . "

You begin to see why the King is an awesome presence? I know this dialogue may seem unduly melodramatic, but it is the King's way of imparting what is, in fact, a densely packed coded message designed to be interpreted later. He has to put across so much, in such a short space of time as his links with me are so tenuous, that as the recipient I need to rely far more on how the message *felt* when it was given than by what was actually said.

By 'power', he means 'light energy' and not that one should wield physical or political power over anybody. Instead, when aspirants come across such spiritual energy they should simply encourage it to grow, and by dedication and service it grows within us all.

'Knights' and 'Ladies' is a code the King uses in conversation, bearing in mind his association with Arthurian legend. It does *not* mean that such people are a social élite. These descriptions are merely titles for budding initiates and specify whereabouts they are on the four main pathways to the Grail. In the end, all titles are meaningless, but we sometimes need to have some kind of label or rank applied to us, for purposes of identification if for no other reason.

'Principal players' are all those who feel deeply that they

have a specific task to undertake in the future, but who have not yet discovered what it may be. Please remember this is not some grandiose idea, or is egocentrically inspired; the King refers to those people who have begun to understand the true meaning of the word 'service'.

The 'amblers and dabblers' are not serious students! The King speaks in this way because he is the archetypal hero, and *we have grown to expect it of him.*

Merlin then spoke to me:

"The number seven has anchored man to the Earth for too long. The reason for the heavy emphasis on sevens during this night of vision is to point out to *you* the end of their sovereignty. The number of the future is eight. If you think in terms of music, the seven notes are an incomplete octave; the eighth note finishes the scale *and* begins the next. With too much emphasis on seven you get locked into the material world. To reach the higher worlds you must move away from seven, otherwise you simply go round and round in circles, getting no-where . . . "

Both energies lingered a little longer then lifted skywards before vanishing from sight and senses.

Subsequently, I have begun to discover what the Mage meant by his reference to the number seven; it is so interesting that it merits a book on its own. Indeed, there are other ideological connections which confirm the importance of octaves – consider, for example, the Buddhist 'Eight-fold Path' and the Cosmic Family of the *I-Ching*.

My next milestone seemed to indicate that at least a part of the King's prophecy was beginning to come true.

'Through the course of many lives you weave a spiral pattern of spiritual energy much like a skein of wool. Some of you get this skein hopelessly tangled and knotted, then spend further lifetimes unravelling the mess you have created. This is all part of the process we call 'perfecting the spirit,' or the 'light within'. It is vitally important that your higher energies operate in perfect harmony. To this end every hour in every day, every day in a year, each year in a lifetime, every life you lead in a millenium, each precious second is a vital part of your quest. Through becoming aware of this fact you begin to quest correctly; thus increasing your perceptions and eventually your spiritual potential.'

M

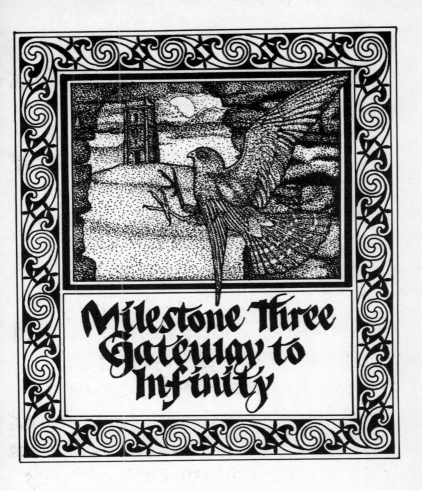

Milestone Three
Gateway to Infinity

My personal inner preparation intensified one summer evening later in 1977, when my wife and I were sitting peacefully at home in the half-light. We heard a sound, like the hem of a robe brushing across the carpet. There was no-one else present, therefore we concentrated upon the area from where the sound had come in order to try and intuit what we should do. My wife suggested we place our chairs in that area of the room. This we did and almost at once I felt an air of expectancy, as if something was about to happen.

As soon as I closed my eyes, I began to feel the dizziness that I associate with the approach of Merlin. Although I was able to communicate freely with my wife throughout what followed, I felt that a part of me had been taken from the room to another dimension altogether.

When my vision cleared, I found myself in a deep blue space. Three Eastern-looking figures appeared before me and bowed low. They exuded love, but of a subtle kind that goes far beyond the emotional. Without warning they proceeded to conjure up every negative thought, dream, nightmare and fantasy I had ever experienced in my life and made me face them squarely, at nose level! I could not avoid looking at what I most feared. Desperately, I clung to the name of my mentor intoning it to myself, like a mantra. My fears vanished.

Then a journey began. Visions flashed past faster and faster as I found myself hurtling through a black tunnel. The tunnel vanished, as suddenly as it had appeared, and I was standing in a room with no doors. It was quite dark. The three figures approached me and bowed low once again. I was told that I had done well and had passed an initiation of some kind.

At first I was too stunned to grasp what all this meant. The room became lighter until I could see that it was panelled up to about eight feet from the ground, octagonal in shape with white walls above the panelling, although I could not look up far enough to see the ceiling. All the light in the place seemed to come from above the panelling.

I projected the full name of my mentor into the room and at once the white segments of the walls came alive with multi-hued movement. Each of the eight facets had its own vibration and shade which seemed to harmonize with the whole. I turned to each light source in turn and bowed low.

Then the second phase began. I was examined in minute detail, like some specimen under the microscope, but in a loving way so that I felt no fear or discomfort. They reached to the very depths of my soul and I stood naked before them, stripped of all pretension. I felt a great surge of relief, like breathing in fresh spring air.

At last they pronounced themselves satisfied. I should explain that we had been communing in a way totally new to me, involving the use of colours and musical sounds rather than words. I seemed to possess an ability to understand this form of communication, but I have never been able to recapture it since. Finally, a light of peace descended upon me and I was asked to undertake several assignments for them, which I readily accepted. I was not permitted to retain complete knowledge of these tasks, however, when I returned to the everyday world.

The three figures approached me again, carrying a plush cushion. I was told that I was to be given a gift. On the cushion lay a crown, a simple circlet of gold. I hoped they were not going to ask me to wear it; but I should have known better. They simply tipped the crown slightly so that I could gaze into it – the gift was a vision!

The face of a dark-haired young man materialised within the crown. He was wearing a T-shirt and was accompanied by a blond, bearded friend who seemed to be his closest companion. I saw that they were seated together in what appeared to be a university or college dining area. The image then changed to that of a golden-haired young woman dressed in a smart three-piece suit. She was at some sort of exhibition, looking at a mercator projection of the globe that was lit from behind. The vision faded and I was back in the sitting room with my wife.

We both felt that I must have crossed some particular personal hurdle. Quite what the vision in the crown meant I have yet to discover fully. However, I feel that there must be some connection with the fact that I went back to college myself in 1981 in order to study for a degree.

I remain grateful for the initiation because of the contentment and reassurance it brought me. I no longer fear the unknown; I have not suffered with nightmares since that time; and I feel easier in my mind knowing that such realms, journeys and beings exist – albeit in other dimensions of time and space.

Yet the initiation was just beginning. About a year later, I made what I believe was a *physical* journey into other realms, which proved to be milestone four.

'You are seeking for ways that lead towards the Light, are you not? The upward path? The secret lies in harmony and balance, both without — and within. Until you can attune to the lovely planetary being who is carrying you across the Celestial Ocean, there can be no going forward. One way to avert the nightmare your leaders are so busy creating for you is to find and awaken the Holy sites venerated by your distant ancestors. These sites are a precious link with the past. We did not seed them for No Purpose! But, having found them, use them with care, use them with Love.'

Milestone Four
Another Time,
Another Place

Like many others, I have become concerned for our world, the very ground under our feet. I long to know how best to serve it, understand it and live in harmony with it. Thanks to the continual prompting of the Magician, I have been fortunate enough to discover energies I had never even considered could exist. I have come to recognise the existence of natural 'order' and numerical 'mean' through the ancient science of 'Geomancy'. I have also witnessed phenomena that can only be explained by the presence of other dimensions altogether.

In his book *The Ancient Science of Geomancy*, Nigel Pennick restores credibility to this old system of alignments and measures, and reminds us how vital this forgotten science of numbers, measures, proportions and harmonies is to our quest for a greater understanding of the Earth and of ourselves.

I owe my first, tenuous links with geomancy to the ancient Chinese oracle – the *I-Ching*. I was introduced to this book by Merlin himself, who physically marched me up to it in a London bookshop! I just had to buy it. Reading through the commentaries that form a central part of the *I-Ching*, I began to realise that I had stepped into a treasure house of knowledge and wisdom whose many doors could lead on to unexplored territories.

I discovered that the Chinese regarded the Earth as a living entity – which makes more and more sense as one attunes oneself to the planet. Subtle energies continually surround and permeate us; others lie beneath our feet in complex patterns. It has been a part of my personal progression to attempt to unravel these patterns and to understand them better. Thanks to the stimulus of my mentor; this work has been sustained ever since.

Practical work really began for me at the time of the winter solstice in 1975, when I felt impressed to attempt an exciting pilgrimage to Saffron Walden in Essex. There, my wife and I found a maze and a series of earthworks that seemed to be linked together in a spiral pattern of spiritual energy.

Since then a picture of a Round Table *has* begun to emerge that spreads across the face of Britain (as the magician explained in Milestone Two). At the same time, patterns in the night sky are found to be reflected on the landscape. Forces seem to wax and wane, like the phases of the moon, and circles and triangles of energy appear to be repeated across the country, echoing the type of energy which each site possesses.

One evening in 1978, I was impressed by my mentor to visit the middle point of a base line drawn across England between two prime sources of energy in the west and east of the country. I was accompanied on this occasion by two friends, who might best be described as interested sceptics.

I had no idea what to expect as we drove through the Buckinghamshire countryside. We arrived at the rather isolated spot, near Stowe School, and parked by a church that loomed in the twilight. It was 8.00 p.m. as we walked towards a long avenue of trees, which I sensed had some connection with the two great sources of power.

As we entered the avenue, a mist began to rise from the grass. The wind was blowing quite fiercely outside, but as we stepped between the two rows of trees, the air was completely still. We could just about hear the tops of the trees being lashed by the gale, but inside was like a natural cathedral. Everything was hushed.

We could see along the entire avenue as we entered, but this was soon obscured by the mist that continued to rise as we walked forward. After a further six to eight paces forward, the mist had come up to our shoulders. Several more paces further and the mist had reached the bottom-most branches of the wind-lashed trees above our heads.

One of our number, Roy Davis, decided to remain where he was and to go no further. His vision in the half-light was not good and in fog was almost non-existent! We left him with a battery powered torch and made our way forward along the avenue as best we could.

The mist itself was silvery blue and very thick, but I could swear that other people passed us from time to time going in the opposite direction. I presumed these to be local people using the public right-of-way.

Eventually, after what seemed an age, we emerged at the far end into the fading light, a high wind and a clear, late-September sky. Looking back from where we had come, we could see that the avenue was still filled with mist; yet

93

either side was perfectly clear and the tops of the trees were being blown about wildly.

My companion became unnerved and decided to walk back along the outside of the avenue in the clear, while I plunged back into the mist. We had estimated that the avenue could not be more than a half-mile long, so a brisk walk should see us back with Roy at the other end in a matter of minutes. My companion said he would call out every few paces and I could reply from within the mist in order to remain in touch.

This time, the silence inside the mist was almost total. I could hear nothing at all and my shouts seemed out of place and curiously muffled. I was rapidly losing all sense of direction, when a line of figures passed me going in the same direction as myself. As they appeared to be carrying lanterns, I latched on behind them.

They were a silent bunch and I had been following them for some time, becoming accustomed to the swish of their long cloaks through the grass. (When I say they carried lanterns I mean to convey the effect of a halo of dim light that surrounded them; I did not see any actual light source as such.) They made little sound as they moved along other than the faint 'swish' and I was just plucking up enough courage to accost the figure nearest to me when my frightened companion cannoned into me from the left. He had become even more alarmed alone, having had no reply to his repeated shouts, and so had dived into the mist to find me.

We scrambled after the now-distant lights and some moments later bumped into Roy who had been waiting patiently for us. He had a strange story to tell; of figures passing by during his lonely vigil in the mist; of how, in order to get his bearings, he had walked across the avenue and emerged on either side into the clear light of dusk. Finally, he had seen us as tiny figures in a tunnel of mist who had not grown any larger or come nearer until we were almost on top of him.

94

We all agreed that we had had enough and consulted our wrist-watches. To our dismay it was 11.00 p.m. so we had missed the closing time of the local pub (which we had noticed on our approach to the area and had estimated was a fifteen-minute drive away) where we had planned to get something to eat on our way home.

As we emerged from the avenue, the mist was dispersing. By the time we were clear of the trees, it had totally disappeared and we could now see all of the way down the long avenue.

Climbing back into the car, we drove off and upon approaching the pub were surprised to see the lights still shining. Hoping for a late-night extension of its opening hours, we entered the crowded bar – and saw that the pub clock showed only 9.15 p.m. We checked our three watches again (two digital, one clockwork); they all read 11.15 p.m.!

Somehow, somewhere, we had gained two hours; or something had accelerated all three watches. How does one begin to explain this?

The only tenable theory is that Merlin had shown us another dimension in which time runs differently from our own. The figures that we had all seen must inhabit that realm, and they had appeared to me as beings surrounded by light.

This incident convinced Roy, at least, that such things are possible. However, my other friend was so frightened that he refused to discuss the incident ever again! Both Roy and I felt that we had seen into – no, more than that – had entered briefly into another world altogether. Perhaps we had passed through an inter-dimensional 'doorway'

Such locations *do* exist. It was a matter of being impressed when to go to one that had enabled us to witness such strange things. Since that time, I have been made aware that we all have the potential means of attuning ourselves to the 'cosmic clock'. Although such unusual conditions are only apparent at certain times, we can learn to interpret when these events are likely to occur and so be on hand to witness them – in the right place and at the right time!

Sadly, I must report that on a recent return visit to the Buckinghamshire site I fould that the trees forming the avenue are dying out. The link between dimensions appears to have moved away as the energies change and rearrange themselves prior to the coming of some new order. What we witnessed could have been some kind of exodus heralding the closing of a door leading from one dimension to another.

What can we learn from this? I believe that we are on the threshold of a deeper understanding of the energies within and around us. Such understanding is vital if we are to redress the many disasterous imbalances in the world. Science alone is *not* enough.

'Many great Truths are
staring you in the face —
the Kingdom of Heaven
is all around, you have
only to open your eyes...'

M

The Song of Songs

You must have noticed many of the dramatic social changes taking place today in the so-called civilized western world? The rapid industrial decline, disappearing hedgerows, destruction of the forests, inner-city decay, grain and butter mountains, fast-junk-food chains, increasing unemployment, drug abuse, alcoholism, chemical pollution and so on?

Compare the above with the natural effects of the planet: tidal waves and droughts; fires and floods; earthquakes and volcanic eruptions. It is almost as if we are creating such catastrophes by our selfish, unthinking treatment of the Earth and the natural landscape. *But not all changes have to be negative ones.*

For the affluent western societies, perhaps the greatest arbiter of change in this century has been its popular music. Since the second World War, music has responded almost more than any other medium to the energy of the times. Popular music has carved out a deep niche in the public consciousness; it is through a blend of words and melody that certain energies and frequencies pertinent to the time are broadcast throughout the world. We all have our favourite tunes. One song in particular that haunted my formative years was Bob Dylan's *The Times They Are A-Changing*. It seemed to capture an essence of the period. Another Dylan song, also recorded by Peter, Paul and Mary, *Blowing in the Wind* expressed a mood which found a deep and responsive vibration within me. I do not think I was alone in this! I have often heard it said since: "These are strange times we're living in . . ."

They appear strange to us because they are times of inexorable change. Things are *going* to change whether we want them to or not! There does not seem to be any way we can avoid it. Nevertheless, I repeat, the changes do *not* have to be bad ones. Dylan's message of different things to come reached into the hearts of a great many people, among them musicians, poets, artists, and philosophers. It is a message of hope that continues to reverberate as later generations take up the torch.

Through our folk-song and popular music we have learned to express our frustrations, because music (like all art forms) has the ability to touch an individual to the depths of their very soul. From time to time such mass emotional links are vital. For example. Elvis, Dylan, Lennon, the Beatles, Buddy Holly, the Rolling Stones, Genesis, Pink Floyd, etc. all have at some point in time, managed to catch an essence of the public mood or consciousness and put it into their music. For many people such performers appear to have so captured that mood that they have amplified it, and by the same token have brought to the surface of many lives an element that had been driven from us in the past – mysticism.

Magic and mysticism were driven out of the lives of the so called civilized societies by Puritan forebears and others of varying religious or political persuasion. They are parts of the human psyche that have been struggling to get back ever since! I am convinced that for many people in the world popular music is re-establishing this missing element. This bodes well for the future, for only a few hundred years ago such a thing could never have happened in Europe without torture and horrific death being the outcome. To-day we are more enlightened. But there is *still* an element of darkness at large in the world, the darkness of ignorance and bigotry. The Magician seems to be indicating that *this* is what is causing the problems with the climate!

Many ordinary people of the world are beginning to understand that we cannot continue as we are at the moment, with the richer nations living at the expense of poorer ones. In the affluent western societies, great mountains of foodstuffs pile up whilst two thirds of the world population remains at starvation level. This cannot go on indefinitely. Indeed, we have begun to see the Earth's natural resources dwindling away. Yet, like Nero, our leaders still seem intent on 'fiddling while Rome burns!' Drastic social changes have to take place; but how?

Through magic and mysticism, and concern for the environment, more and more people are becoming sensitive to the plight of our planet. Through popular music and by active involvement in causes, they are becoming aware that there is a greater plan for humanity than simply frittering away a precious existence in petty squabbling, and selfishness and exploitation of our world's resources. Through the auspices of popular music and other artistic media, higher influences are getting through to very many people. One might ask, why, then, does such an influence not strike at the very heart of our societies and contact our leaders directly? To me the answer is, primarily, because our leaders are 'drunk' from the effects of power. (Have *you* ever tried talking some sense into a drunk?) Secondly, so-called leaders will not be affected because *we* are the ones who have to change the system willingly, and not have it imposed upon us from above.

We have to accept our individual responsibilities before anything can truly change for the better on any larger scale. If we do *not* make the right decisions, then inevitably I think we will condemn ourselves to slow extinction: it is as simple as that.

I believe that great changes are taking place in the cosmos, and we either move with them or get left behind. We may not be alone in the Universe, and there may be Guardians looking after the Earth. Nevertheless, on our world we all live under the threat of nuclear annihilation. Have we a future to look forward to, or are we destined to be utterly destroyed?

The following further treasury of Merlin's words offers us more than a glimmer of hope. He has indicated that through stringent, self-examination we might have a chance of a secure world, free of tension and discord. The key to a brighter future lies with us.

*   *   *

"You cannot begin to conceive of the powers involved in creating a Universe, and it is all intelligently controlled. Compared with such powers the puny efforts of a few power-hungry fools on Earth pale into insignificance. Make no mistake, a period of testing and tempering is underway and the influence of the other planets in the Solar System, when acting like a series of giant electro-magnets, will be very great indeed. Be prepared for great changes, particularly on the consciousness level . . ."

"You must know that it is possible for us to remove all traces of the Earth from the Universe if we wish. There is a power in the cosmos that can enclose the Earth in a 'blanket', fold it up, and remove it forever. But such power is not within the realms of matter at all and can never be attained by physical man . . ."

"Drive from your mind any fears of arrogant scientists or military despots completely destroying the Earth. The great Earth Mother has her own scale of time, and she is slow to react when compared with the turmoil of mankind; but she will react to massive abuses of her eco-systems – just wait and see! Do not fear too much for the Earth, she has many safety devices that can negate the destructive elements of industry and agriculture in the long term. But this does mean that mankind is able to wreak havoc in the short term, usually at a greater cost to himself."

"Never imagine that you will ever create the perfect society in the physical world. Your material world is a classroom, to which you return again and again, you are in it to learn. In order that you do learn it has to be possible for you to make mistakes, and you cannot do that in a 'perfect world'. Such an ideal is impossible at the level of your present existence. To progress towards a state of perfection it is necessary for you to be sensitive to the possibility of differences of opinion about any situation. No two individuals can agree totally upon what they think they see, for example. Always be aware that it is the negative experiences in life that teach you most; if your world was 'perfect' then the learning experience would be almost non-existent. This is why your physical world is like it is; we are not saying there is no room for improvement though! Improvement comes from within the individual. What we are seeking is for you to understand the lessons being taught in your classroom and to learn from them. Sadly, many of you do not seem to be aware of the classroom at all; and those who are aware do not seem to be paying much attention to the lessons, let alone the teachers! A greater sense of self-discipline is essential; discipline of the mind, the body and the spirit. Increased social awareness will grow from this – as a direct consequence of working on the self."

"A great many social problems are basically sexual ones. Men fear women, and women in turn fear men. As a direct consequence young people are afraid to touch one another; in some cases are afraid even to approach one another for fear that their actions be misconstrued. Your attitudes towards sex are changing, gradually, but they are terribly prudish – even now! A more open approach to the whole subject of sex and relationships must be a priority in any future society. Equality in all discussions and decision-making will assist in creating a more favourable atmosphere between the sexes."

"Drastic changes have to take place in your economic, political and religious systems if the present imbalances are to be checked. Drastic reassessment of agrarian policies and techniques have to occur before the damage becomes to great to repair. Make no mistake, excessive mountains of food cannot be allowed to accumulate leaving two-thirds of the world's population to starve. It is morally inexcusable for anyone to exploit the staff of life; it breaks every rule in the humanitarian canon of belief. These changes will occur – if only those who hold a degree of power, as yet untested and untried, begin to wield it."

"Political and social chicanery has been going on for centuries, perpetuated by groups of secret societies who are anxious to hold on to the reins of power. God, too, has become a marketable commodity, to be 'sold' by the privileged few! But remember, God is everywhere; this stranglehold will pass away if only more of you can become aware of God's presence all around you."

"Bloodlines continue to be an obsession with some people and their secret associations. Mistakenly they believe that mixing bloodlines weakens the stock. If anything, your history shows the reverse to be true. This obsession goes back a long way, to the time of the existence of the 'true sight', and those who believed that they could own this ability, hold on to it and prevent others from achieving it. Such is not possible, although these groups have tried every trick in their books to gain their ends. You are all in the physical world to learn, to mix, to live in peace with one another. If you accept the idea of reincarnation then why should one racial group matter above another? You will experience all races and human conditions during the course of your many lives. This makes a nonsense of the whole ideal of bloodlines or race."

"Every human body is beautiful and should be regarded as being splendidly unique to you for the time you inhabit it. Too often, though, a false image of human perfection is created in the public consciousness. Failure to live up to this standard (artificial though it is) leads to frictions, tensions – even shame! Why should nudity be regarded as sinful? Why is it thought to encourage promiscuity? Why is it such a joke? It is often embarrassing in the Western world for one person to view another naked. Such extreme reactions are used to cover deeper emotions, such as social shame and prudishness with regard to the act of procreation. You have been conditioned into thinking of sex as 'dirty'. This shame and fear of the body is soon transmitted to your children. Youngsters in their innocence often show how society should work. Jungle tribes, too, often have more well-balanced social orders and sensible attitudes to sex and the body. However, if you introduce a 'cultured' person into their lives their bodies are covered up in rapid time. Why? Ask yourself why you are so afraid of anything to do with sex or your body, why you get so embarrassed, why you would not choose to change your clothing in public? Is it because you are caught in the erroneous belief that sex is dirty or depraved or disgusting?"

"It is essential to cultivate a responsible attitude where sex is concerned. Unlicensed deviant behaviour is a direct result of the ultra-severe moral strictures imposed by all sorts of religious bigots over the centuries. They have created more sexual problems than they have tried to prevent . . . Sex is not going to go away. It is a vital part of your physical existence – the continuation of life. You have to find a sexual balance that suits you, and your partner, but try to avoid extremes of thought or action. The sexually balanced society is not going to appear overnight, but changes for the better are taking place gradually. Contraception is slowly being accepted as a valid means of controlling the size of the population. It is not wrong to prevent unwanted pregnancies if your circumstances are such that a child could suffer if brought into the world. However, this does not shelve the responsibility completely. Thoughtless sexual unions still produce unwanted children, and uncaring attitudes creep in; sexual education is off-loaded onto 'someone else' and the cycle is perpetuated. How are young people to develop a sense of sexual responsibility if the whole subject is taboo, or no-one cares enough to explain it all to them?

"If your society considered rationally, any unwanted children would find ready and loving homes with childless couples, but very often parents are forced to keep a child they do not want, or cannot take adequate care of, because 'official' social morality demands it. Yet your social and sexual morality can change like the fashions in clothing! The whole subject is an enigma. Those who have sex on demand, with a constant supply of different partners, tire of it and seek deviations; those who are denied sex often commit violent acts of an aberrant kind too. It is essential that a balance prevails in the union of the sexes; open communication and a tolerant attitude is becoming more apparent and there is hope for the future, but there are dark clouds that still need to be cleared away."

"For far too long the predatory male has lusted after every female, and then blamed her for arousing him! The woman is blamed for 'seducing' him, for submitting to him or for *not* submitting to him! In consequence she is then labelled a whore, a tart, 'easy', frigid, prudish, or even a 'tease'. Having sown his 'wild oats', our hero then expects to marry a virgin! Should a woman show such predatory instincts she is regarded as loose-moralled and unprincipled, even a threat to society. Whence do such attitudes spring? Look no further than the patriarchal religions or societies, like the Judaic, Christian or Islamic ones that dominate the world today; all give the male licence to regard women as legitimate property to be used or abused at will. It is religious dogma that has created many social imbalances and it continues to encourage conflict between the sexes all over the world. Any religion that promotes imbalance must be regarded with suspicion. Try to create a balance in all your sexual, social and spiritual relationships. Loving, caring and sharing should be the key words in any relationship between men and women."

"Love is a key that can unlock many doors, but too often lust is mistaken for it in your physical world. If you could only make yourself more sensitive to the feelings of others such problems would not occur so frequently."

"Becoming a parent involves the ultimate in self-sacrifice. No-one should bring a child into the world unless they are prepared to put themselves last. Marriage should be regarded as a divine state entered into for a physical lifetime, and not undertaken lightly. Too often, sexual desire alone is mistaken for love. In these cases marriage should not be entertained. Free love among consenting people who understand their desires should be an acceptable alternative – this is not 'sinful' at all, just sensible! Children are a precious gift to a marriage, to be treasured in the embrace of a united family, and not regarded as a liability or burden upon their parents. Parenthood is an enormous responsibility, and one that requres a special union in order to produce the desired balance and true happiness. Sexual urges should not be overlooked or suppressed; couples could live together long before even contemplating the commitment of marriage if they entertain any doubts about their partnership (provided both parties agree). True marriage is a bond for life."

"Education is not confined to the schoolroom. A parent should not seek to off-load all responsibility for child-rearing onto the schoolteacher. Each one of you is constantly learning. Remember, your world is one enormous classroom, you cannot avoid or opt out of this process until you have learned all the lessons that life has to teach. Some try, but they merely have to start all over again until they get it right."

"True love and compassion are the most potent energies you possess, yet you choose to overlook them. Your helpers and guides in the other realms are pure LOVE energy. They elect to stay by you to watch over you and teach you in order to progress to higher frequencies on the great Octave themselves. They make both sorts of experience possible for you through a pre-arranged programme that is agreed with you before your birth; due consideration being made by you for the karmic debts you have incurred throughout your various lifetimes. Remember, Peace and Love start within you. First learn to love yourself and forgive your physical nature for you are not expected to be perfect, then you will begin to find peace inside and find the ability to bring this out into your everyday life, and eventually to the world."

"The Kingdom of Heaven is all around you. Your guides and teachers exist in the realms of Spirit. They have chosen to put in your way both positive and negative experiences, these reverberate on many different levels of your existence. How you cope with these on the physical plane governs the reactions that take place higher up the scale. Always keep in mind that physical man can never step into the higher realms for he is composed of the wrong type of energy. However, higher forms of energy can and do come down to you as visions, dreams, symbols, myths or even physical manifestations from time to time. Material man cannot be permitted total knowledge, or ultra-deep insights into the Great Plan. Although scraps of information are filtered down whenever possible, the scope is too great for his mind to encompass. Sadly, a lot of information becomes processed by the recipient into something warped or distorted, but some gems do get through to help those who need them."

"The human mind is a formidable force. It is capable of creating anything it wants. Unscrupulous people have imposed their own ideals upon the majority for centuries. Remember, your present concept of 'reality' is actually an illusion. You have accepted a system of existence without question; by so doing you perpetuate it. You have the ability to change it, do not sit about waiting to be 'rescued'! You have only to decide to live your life to the pattern you choose, and nobody can order you to do otherwise. If you want a happy life then simply say to yourself "I am going to live a happy life" – then live it! Do not accept anything blindly, always question . . . but remember others have the right to question you too, and to choose their own way to a happy life."

"A great deal of nonsense has been spoken about the degeneration of races. You must understand that mankind has always had a choice. A soul chooses to face certain tests before it enters the physical body; it is a measure of success or failure how the culture it embraces progresses or declines. Each soul is an integral part of the energy of the race for the time that it spends in the physical world."

"Sensitivity is a double-edged sword. It opens up channels to your higher self and brings back memories of how things could and should be in the material world; this can become more and more frustrating. Your forward-vision will improve and, in consequence, you will see the solutions to problems which others will be unable to appreciate, or will refuse to acknowledge. You will find your pathway getting lonelier the more you progress. Do not despair. Such periods of solitude are necessary initiations, and can be of swift or extended duration – depending on you, and how you cope. Cultivate patience and tolerance of those who oppose your views; find subtle ways to impart your ideas, and then maybe you will be able to solve those problems actively without having to wade through apparent apathy.'

"In the fullness of time you will return to your spiritual home, to the worlds of higher vibration. You are expected to carry back with you the knowledge and experience you have acquired on Earth. Those who have been working for others, rather than for themselves alone, contribute far more of value to the cosmic memory banks than those who have been absorbed in self. However, all information, positive and negative alike, is put to good use towards the guidance and evolution of the greater galaxy; for nothing is ever wasted!"

"Never forget, we need you to dream. It is good for you to dream and use your imagination. Too many souls return to source with little or nothing to offer in the way of self-expression or self-realisation – even from the dream state. In your so-called sophistication it has become an irrelevance to dream, or to enjoy adventures of the mind. Worse, you subject yourselves to increasing sensory assault. I urge you to set aside a few moments each day when you can shut off the relentless bombardment of television, radio and the cacophony of everyday noise; for it is in this private oasis that you carve out for yourself that your inner-self will blossom and grow."

"How long is it since you experienced – really experienced – a sunrise or sunset? How often do you find yourself walking along with downcast eyes? Look up, look around you; experience the beauty, the intelligence and design, the humour of nature everywhere – even in cities, where you least expect to find it."

"I have told you that new energies are being released onto the Earth. They are designed to help you in whatever you do, and to help you find your way back to your own personal path when you discover you have strayed or been side-tracked. Do not believe the media-created life-lies. Be yourself! Be truly honest for just a few moments each day; see yourself and the world around you with unclouded eyes – it will pay huge dividends."

"Your future must contain a privileged place within it for the elderly and the very young. Any nation or person who neglects the old and denies the young deserves nothing but contempt. You were all young once and you will all grow old – there is no way to avoid this transition. It is a natural progression. But your present world values only those who are able-bodied, who can produce the 'gross national product'. Think, what has it produced? Look around you at all the dissatisfied faces. Is this paradise?"

"The elderly and infirm should always elicit your care, sympathy and responsibility. How do you expect to be treated when you are old? Give a thought to your own declining years before turning away from the plight of those who cannot always fight for themselves, or provide the essentials of life through waning strength and limited incomes. Should you harbour any resentment in your heart towards the old then you will one day be shown the degree and extent of your shame. Deny the weak, the unprotected and the senior members of your community, and you deny God!"

'Remember, you are not alone.
We are always with you.
Open your eyes and see;
listen and you will hear.
Still your mind and the
Truth can begin to flood in.
This is all we ask of you.'

The Drama we Call Life

"All the world's a stage,
And all the men and women merely players:
They have their exits and their entrances;
And one man in his time plays many parts . . ."

William Shakespeare *As You Like It*

This is a great truth: drama is an essential part of our human behavioural system. Every day we are constantly rôle-playing; whether at home, at the place of work, at parties, and social events or at the shops or market. Take a good look at yourself: you will realise that you have many 'faces', or masks' that you wear during the day. Life, as we now know it, has become a series of unco-ordinated 'acts'. We no longer acknowledge that we *are* performing. But for whom are we performing? What characters are we playing? Will we ever discover who we *really* are?

Look at the example of the Ancient Greeks. They were highly aware of the subtle influences of drama in their lives, celebrating the art as a religious festival in honour of their god Dionysus (whose Roman equivalent was Bacchus, as we have seen).

Bacchanalian celebrations were traditionally held at a time which coincides with Yuletide and the modern Christmas. Today, those who still perform, plays and pantomines, and who throw parties in the 'Festive Season', never acknowledge the fourth, or Dionysian energy that is present at such events. Any professional actor will tell you that a play (or 'piece') has an energy all of its own. Certain characters from the classics contain this energy also; the very act of performance seems to trigger off this energy between the actor and the audience as they share in the intimacy of an act of Creation. It is a thing of the moment; fleeting; transient. Yet some plays are more effective in this way than others; some characters, too, lend themselves more readily to the creation of such energy. So it is in Life.

This is what the Dionysian element of performance is all about. It can be wild at times, even disorderly if not properly understood or channelled correctly. Yet it is *not* to be feared. We must understand that this energy is an integral part of human nature. It maintains our creativity. Nevertheless, as I have already indicated, it is only *one facet* of a more complicated whole. I have come to believe that there are *four* major energies within us. As I have indicated, in order to make them easier to comprehend, I have been forced to anthropomorphize them into characters; 'The Magician', 'The King', 'The Holy Lady', and 'The Mystic'.

Interestingly, science has also begun to show that there are four basic energies that make up the building blocks of the Universe; gravity, electro-magnetism, strong atomic force, and weak atomic force. (The strong atomic force is that which holds atoms and molecules together: the weak atomic force is what keeps them apart so that they can vibrate).

This pattern of 'four' echoes and re-echoes throughout the whole gamut of human experience. I believe it also colours our subconscious thinking. C.G. Jung brought this into finer focus in his study *Archetypes of the Collective Unconscious.*

Why *do* we have recurrent themes running through our literature, our dreams, our art, our religion and our daily lives? Is there a pool of collective energy in the Universe that manifests in four major ways? I like to think there is; I call it 'God'. It is my contention that we are essentially made up from a combination of these four energies of God. However, *we continually make the mistake of worshipping one of them to the detriment of all the others.*

Think about the space we inhabit; it is three-dimensional, with time being a possible fourth dimension. Our bodies, too, are three-dimensional in form and subject to the subtle changes worked through time. Lots of 'fours' in the physical world.

Now consider the religious aspects: in the Christian story of Mary and Jesus, rather than the supposed trinity, there are four major archetypes present: Jesus (the King), Mary (Holy Lady), God the Father (the Magician), and Satan or Saturn (the Mystic).

This story has played a large part in Western culture, and yet M.H. Tester in his book *But What Do We Tell The Children?* shows how the virgin birth story is a much-loved and much-used one through many ages. Jesus was apparently the *seventeenth* Christ to appear in human history. We seem to need such hero figures to look up to and follow as a shining example, but this, again is only one quarter of the whole picture. There were *four* key figures in this mythology and, of course, *four* Evangelists – ultimately! In the Old Testament, in *Genesis*, we find Adam and Eve with their two offspring Cain and Abel.

Consider too the Arthurian Romances. There is Merlin (the Magician), Arthur (the doomed warrior/king), the Holy Lady in triple guise – (Guinivere – modelled on Eve-, Morgan-le-Fey, and the Lady of the Lake) finally Mordred/ Lancelot (the reluctant destroyer). Four major figures again.

Of course, one could point to the four seasons, the four winds, the four cardinal points, the four faces of Brahma, the four streams of paradise, the four elements, the four corners of the Earth and the four horsemen of the Apocalypse! There are many, many indications of 'four' in religion and mythology, suggesting the different major influences.

Consider music for a moment. Western music is grouped in scales, or octaves, which contain eight major notes and thirteen chromatic notes. I contend that the eight major notes could be a doubling up of the four energies, or a breaking down of the four into their constituent vibratory parts.

From my investigations into music and the human shape, I have found that we appear to have thirteen areas of the body that could be regarded as notes in our personal 'octaves', which in turn are probably collections of further octaves in different frequencies. There are only six full tones in any octave of music. The six tones of the human octave would seem, therefore, to represent the archetypal body of a six-foot man. If we share these proportions between the four energies we discover that one-and-a-half tones would seem to be the equivalent of one energy influence. One-and-a-half feet is the equivalent of that ancient measurement, the cubit. The ratio of 1:1½ is that of the tonic to the dominant note (in the same musical scale) and of the foot to the cubit. Before you scoff and dismiss such notions as crazy, consider the building recommendations pertaining to staircases: a

116

staircase must have at least thirteen steps (not twelve). Research has shown that if this code is not adhered to then people keep falling downstairs! Could it be that our lives *are* governed by frequencies? Or energies?

Let us consider the old 'Northern' foot of 13.2 inches. It is thought to be at least 5000 years old and was once in regular use throughout Europe and the East. My attention was drawn to this measurement by the Mage in 1977. At that time, I had no evidence to suggest that such a measurement ever existed. Ten years later, a friend found the proof for me in O'Keefe's *Weights and Measures* and sent me a copy. Naturally, I was delighted! If we compare this 'foot' with musical frequencies, we find that at an octave below middle C, the note vibrates at 132 hertz or cycles per second. When we then discover that 13.2 inches (1.1 ft.) just so happens to be the rate that the speed of sound increases if the temperature rises by 1 degree Centigrade, we begin to see subtle connections between certain measurements and music.

What can we deduce from all this evidence? It may seem circumstantial but we have to assume that the drama we call 'Life' does have some ultimate purpose; that there once was a connection through measurement to an underlying pattern, frequency, plan or script that has been lost, or forgotten. Perhaps land measures were once harmonics of natural energy. I feel we should be looking for more evidnece of the old script to try and find out where we fit into the present scenario! We should be seeking to find out what part we are expected to play. The Celestial Directors make their stage directions known through the unexpected things that happen to us in the course of our daily lives, but most of us are too blind to see. We do not always heed them, much less respond correctly. *We have to learn to accept the rôles assigned to us.* This is not an easy process, as I know from bitter personal experience! Yet it can become easier if we try and play our 'scenes' honestly, without pretending we are something or someone we are not. Our first task is honesty with ourselves; accepting both our strengths and our weaknesses. Then we have to find the part of the 'Cosmic Script' that applies to us.

None of this is easy. There are many problems if one decides to undertake such a task; unscrupulous people have tried to destroy the original script over the ages. Others have tried to hide it, edit it, change it, or to destroy all knowledge of it. They have very nearly succeeded in the latter case, which makes our task doubly difficult. Yet in spite of all this, the drama continues, for the show must go on.

We have to determine whether we are back-stage material, supporting cast or a principal player. We must then *accept* our allocated rôles in the knowledge that through the course of many lives the time will come for us to hold the centre of the stage. Sadly, all too few of us show any aptitude for such acceptance, or any awareness that we may be fated to spend our lives as the equivalent of playing in a provincial theater! It is obvious to me that we cannot *all* occupy the main stage in world events; it would collapse under the strain. Yet, some people force their way onto that arena long before their time or their 'cue' – with disastrous consequences.

It is of paramount importance that we recognise the significance of this 'drama' in our lives. The knowledge will help us to see what is illusion and what is reality. The scenery around us seems real enough, yet some of our fellow players are hell-bent on wrecking the set because it does not conform to some artificial construct they have built up from gross misinterpretation of a phoney script. If they could but pause, and stop taking themselves and their act so seriously, they might just catch a glimpse of the *real* drama taking place.

Once a performer begins to realise just what the original play is all about, then he or she can begin the arduous task of understanding the 'scenes'. It does not stop there, however, for major problems occur when one is approaching the end of an 'act' (or the end of an Era), for this marks a major transition of the play. It is a period of time when there are complete shifts in emphasis, leading on to new themes or new territory.

Ultimately, our part in this play is about our journey – or rather the soul's journey – towards the reunion that occurs when: 'What is above and what is below are of one mind' (Ralph Blum *The Book of Runes*). Each of us has to ask what constitutes 'right action'. Once our stage directions are clear then we can begin to neutralize our refusal to let right action flow through us.

Through my adventures with the Magician, I feel that I have found a part of the Cosmic Script which applies to me. A four-fold vision, much like the one described by William Blake:

> *Now I a fourfold vision see,*
> *And a fourfold vision is given to me;*
> *'Tis fourfold in my supreme delight*
> *And threefold in soft Beulah's night*
> *And twofold always. May God us keep*
> *From single vision and Newton's sleep.*

It is 'single vision and Newton's sleep' that has brought us almost to the brink of destruction. Yet many well-intentioned folk *still* believe that a Saviour or a Celestial Director of somekind will appear in the nick of time and put everything right again! Let me hasten to disabuse anyone that the Magician has confirmed such a concept. On the contrary, in our dialogues together, he has intimated that *we* have to get it right this time; though we will receive occasional advice from the odd dialogue coach or stage manager. Yet how will this come about?

As you are now aware, I have come to believe that the four basic energies of the Universe are contained within our subconscious as archetypal images, as well as being part of our physical make-up. I believe that there are a variety of symbols which can be triggered in us when sympathetic cosmic or earth vibrations are present.

The writer Geoffrey Ashe believes that a lot of major psychic and spiritual 'triggers' stem from hidden sources like Shambala. I have no quarrel with such a concept. Indeed, it echoes an initiation I have described elsewhere in this book. I believe there are other-world beings, here to help us, foregoing their own development to stay closer to the human race in order to try and reach us with stimulating ideas. Strangely, their contact with us varies in intensity, like the signal from a fading and recurring distant radio station. I feel it is thanks to such groups – dialogue coaches and stage managers in the play – that the experiences I have enjoyed are possible. They assist in building connections between this physical world and the spiritual realms. The Merlin energy explained on a number of occasions that it could not have reached me without the assistance of such a group of 'spiritual switchboard operators'.

I consider that it is largely due to such groups that certain music is composed and books of philosophy are written. For example, the ancient Chinese classics the *I-Ching* and the *Tao Te Ching* cannot be attributed authentically to any single author. The name Lao Tsu (or Lao Tse) often connected with the Tao simply means 'Old Master'; not the name of a specific person. No one can say for sure who wrote either of these masterful classics, but one of the key tenets (Number 25) in the *Tao Te Ching* perhaps gives us a clue:

"Something mysteriously formed, born before Heaven and
  Earth,
In the silence and the void. Standing alone and unchanging,
Ever present and in motion.
Perhaps it is the Mother of the ten thousand things?
I do not know its name. Call it Tao.
For lack of a better word, I call it great.
Being great it flows. It flows far away.
Having gone far, it returns.
Therefore, 'Tao is great; Heaven is great; Earth is great;
The King is also great.'
These are the four great powers of the Universe,
And the King is one of them.
Man follows the Earth. Earth follows Heaven.
Heaven follows the Tao. The Tao follows what is natural."

Lao Tsu (my italics)

It is my personal belief that the Tao comes as close to the
Cosmic Script as it is possible to get. I believe that the
future is governed by our ability to return to an awareness of
the Tao; a return to an awareness of the Cosmic Script; a
return to what is natural.

Merlin's Prayer
'May the light of Peace,
Joy and love,
be with you now,
and for ever more...'

Bibliography

The works listed below are those referred to in the text and are principally the U.K. editions as used by the author. In some instances, simply out of useage and reference by the author, a later paperback edition of a work is cited rather than the original hardback.

Ashe, Geoffrey *Camelot and the Vision of Albion* Heinemann, London 1970.

Ashe, Geoffrey *The Quest for Arthur's Britain* Paladin, London 1971.

Ashe, Geoffrey *The Ancient Wisdom* Heinemann, London 1977.

Blake, William *The Complete Poems* Penguin, London 1981.

Blum, Ralph *The Book of Runes* Michael Joseph, London 1982.

Bradley, Marion *The Mists of Avalon* Michael Joseph, London 1983.

Joyce, Donovan *The Jesus Scroll* Sphere, London 1975.

Jung, C.G. *Archetypes and the Collective Unconscious* R.K.P., London 1969.

Lao Tsu *Tai Te Ching* Wildwood House, London 1975.

Lethbridge, T.C. *A Step in The Dark* R.K.P., London 1967.

Lewis, C.S. *That Hideous Strength* Pan, London 1972.

Lincoln, H., Leigh, R. & Baigent, M. *The Holy Blood and The Holy Grail* Jonathan Cape, London 1982.

Lincoln, H., Leigh, R. & Baigent, M. *The Messianic Legacy* Jonathan Cape, London 1986.

Michell, John *The New View Over Atlantis* Thames & Hudson, London 1986.

O'Keefe, John Alfred (ed.) *Laws of Weights and Measures* Butterworth, London 1977.

Pennick, Nigel *The Ancient Science of Geomancy* Thames & Hudson, London 1979.

Powys, John Cowper *A Glastonbury Romance* Picador, London 1975.

Shakespeare, William *The Complete Works* Cassell, London 1958.

Stewart, Mary *The Crystal Cave* Hodder & Stoughton London 1970.

Stewart, Mary *The Hollow Hills* Hodder & Stoughton London 1974.

Stewart, Mary *The Last Enchantment* Hodder & Stoughton London 1979.

Temple, Robert *The Sirius Mystery* Sidgwick & Jackson London 1976.

Tester, M.H. *But What Do We Tell The Children?* Psychic Press, London 1976.

Tolkien, J.R.R. *The Hobbit* Allan & Unwin, London 1971.

Tolkien, J.R.R. *The Lord of the Rings* Allan & Unwin 1971.

Underwood, Guy *Pattern of the Past* Museum Press, London 1969.

Watkins, Alfred *The Old Straight Track* Garnstone, London 1970.

Wilhelm, Richard *The I-Ching (Book of Changes)* R.K.P., London 1975.

Index

The author and illustrator have produced other titles of related interest:
Merlin the Immortal Peter Quiller and Courtney Davis, 1984.
The Celtic Art of Courtney Davis Courtney Davis, 1985.
The Celtic Art Source Book Courtney Davis, 1988.

The Celtia Catalogue is available from Courtney Davis at Woodbine Cottage, Newcause, Buckfastleigh, South Devon TQ11 0AZ, U.K.

In addition, write to Firebird Books Ltd or their distributor, for details of their other publications, including the biographies of four ancient Celtic Warriors.